100 HEURISTICS & HEURISTIC MODELS

100 HEURISTIC MODELS

BY DAN WAITE

BRANCH AND BOUND	VORONOI	MANHATTAN DISTANCE
A* SEARCH	MINIMAX	METAHEURISTICS
SERIAL POSITION	CONTEXT-DEPENDENT	MNEMONIC
RETRIEVAL FLUENCY	SPACED REPETITION	CHUNKING
ADVERSE SELECTION	RULE CHAINING HEURISTIC	MEANS-ENDS ANALYSIS
NORM-FOLLOWING	IN-GROUP BIAS	LEFT-HAND RULE
LEFT-HAND RULE	NAVIGATION AND SPATIAL	EUCLIDEAN DISTANCE
SALIENCE	BASE RATE NEGLECT	AND MANY, MANY MORE

100 HEURISTICS AND HEURISTIC MODELS
BY DAN WAITE

100 HEURISTICS AND HEURISTIC MODELS

BY DAN WAITE

Published by LOCO TEMPUS LIMITED 2025

Cover design by Dan Waite

British Library Cataloguing in Publication Data

A catalogue record for this book is available from the British Library

ISBN: 978-1-917784-18-4

ISBN 978-1-9177841-8-4

9 781917 784184 >

Dan Waite here, CEO of Better Noise Music.

HEURISTICS are something that I have become interested in over the last couple of years after listening to several of Rory Sutherland's videos.

When I went to try and learn more, I realised that it was an untapped area and no one had covered this topic.

I started looking into **HEURISTICS** and quickly realised that there was a lot more to it than I realised and I have enjoyed researching this book very much.

I hope you will also enjoy and be able to apply some of the **HEURISTICS AND HEURISTIC MODELS** within the book.

Good luck on your journey of self-education.

My best,

Dan Waite

This is dedicated to my wife Irena, my family & friends and work colleagues, present and past.

With thanks to Ade Adeluwoye, Nicolas Bate, Sir Richard Branson, Allen Kovac for your trust and guidance as a boss and mentor and Napolean Hill for the advice in spotting opportunity in hard work.

Thank you to inspirational contacts who as a result of their books and classes have me thinking differently, they are Rory Sutherland and Will Page.

In memory of my father David Waite.

Cognitive Heuristics

1. Availability heuristic

2. Representativeness heuristic

3. Anchoring and adjustment

4. Recognition heuristic

5. Fluency heuristic

6. Affect heuristic

7. Take-the-best heuristic

8. Default heuristic

9. Simulation heuristic

10. Familiarity heuristic

Judgment and Decision-Making Heuristics

11. Elimination by aspects

12. Satisficing

13. Fast and frugal trees

14. One-reason decision making

15. Escalation of commitment heuristic

16. Loss aversion heuristic

17. Framing heuristic

18. Status quo heuristic

19. Equity heuristic

20. Mental accounting

AI and Computer Science Heuristics

21. A* search heuristic

22. Minimax heuristic

23. Hill climbing

24. Beam search heuristic

25. Simulated annealing

26. Genetic algorithm fitness heuristic

27. Greedy algorithm

28. Heuristic pruning

29. Tabu search

30. Heuristic function in constraint satisfaction

Search and Optimization Heuristics

31. Divide and conquer

32. Backtracking

33. Iterative deepening

34. Gradient descent (with heuristic tuning)

35. Nearest neighbour heuristic

36. Metaheuristics

37. Subgoal decomposition

38. Rule-of-thumb estimates

39. Branch and bound heuristic

40. Upper/lower bound estimation

💻 Economic & Behavioural Heuristics

41. Endowment effect heuristic

42. Price-quality heuristic

43. Scarcity heuristic

44. Social proof heuristic

45. Heuristic value estimation

46. Compromise effect

47. Default bias

48. Temporal discounting heuristic

49. Decoy effect

50. Habit-based heuristics

Scientific Reasoning Heuristics

51. Parsimony (Occam's razor)

52. Causal heuristic

53. Base rate neglect

54. Confirmation bias heuristic

55. Availability cascade

56. Relevance heuristic

57. Analogy heuristic

58. Hypothesis matching

59. Narrative coherence

60. Salience heuristic

Navigation and Spatial Heuristics

61. Straight-line heuristic

62. Left-hand rule (maze solving)

63. Landmark-based navigation

64. Turn minimizing heuristic

65. Euclidean distance heuristic

66. Voronoi heuristic

67. Waypoint heuristic

👥 Social and Communication Heuristics

💼 Practical/Problem-Solving Heuristics

84. Substitution heuristic

85. Use of analogies

86. Heuristic simplification

87. Rule chaining

88. Chunking

89. Divide big problem into small problems

90. "If it works, don't fix it" heuristic

Learning & Memory Heuristics

91. Spaced repetition heuristic

92. Retrieval fluency heuristic

93. Heuristic cue association

94. Mnemonic heuristics

95. "Testing effect" heuristic

96. Context-dependent recall

97. First impression heuristic

98. Recency heuristic

99. Frequency-based heuristic

100. Serial position heuristic

CHAPTERS

🧠 **Cognitive Heuristics**

1. Availability heuristic

The *availability heuristic* is a mental shortcut in which people estimate the likelihood of an event based on how easily examples come to mind. First introduced by **Tversky and Kahneman (1973)**, this heuristic suggests that judgments about frequency or probability are biased by the *retrievability* of instances, not actual statistical data.

Example

If someone recently saw news about airplane crashes, they might overestimate the risk of flying. Even if statistically flying is safer than driving, the vividness and emotional impact of the crash make it more *available* in memory, skewing perception.

Why It Works

It works because the human brain is efficient but limited in processing vast or abstract data. Rather than calculating objective probabilities, we lean on what's accessible in memory. Our minds assume that if something can be recalled easily, it must be important or common. This evolved strategy helps us make quick decisions in uncertain environments, especially when time or cognitive resources are constrained.

How It Works

The availability heuristic operates through a two-stage process:

1. **Retrieval Cue**: An event or concept (e.g., "How dangerous is flying?") triggers a search in memory.
2. **Ease of Recall**: The brain evaluates how quickly and vividly related examples are retrieved. If many instances come to mind quickly, the brain concludes that the event is frequent or likely.

Emotional intensity, recent exposure, and media coverage can all increase the availability of an event in memory, thereby inflating its perceived likelihood.

Application

In **public health**, the availability heuristic can be used to **encourage preventive behaviours**. For instance, anti-smoking campaigns often highlight emotionally charged stories (e.g., a young cancer patient) rather than statistics. These vivid anecdotes make the dangers of smoking more mentally available, motivating behavioural change more effectively than abstract data.

Conversely, marketers exploit it by flooding consumers with repeated ads or dramatizing product benefits, making the brand top-of-mind and thus more likely to be chosen.

Key Insights

- Availability is not accuracy: Just because something is easy to recall doesn't mean it's statistically common.
- The media amplifies availability bias by disproportionately covering rare, emotionally charged events.

- It explains widespread misjudgements—like overestimating crime rates or underestimating health risks based on anecdotal evidence.
- Awareness of this heuristic can improve critical thinking and help in de-biasing decisions, especially in fields like law, medicine, and finance.
Ultimately, the availability heuristic reflects the brain's tradeoff between speed and precision—powerful, but prone to systematic error when memory and reality diverge.

2. Representativeness heuristic

The *representativeness heuristic* is a mental shortcut where people judge the probability or frequency of an event based on how much it resembles the typical case, rather than using statistical reasoning. Introduced by **Tversky and Kahneman (1972)**, it plays a major role in decision-making under uncertainty. This heuristic relies on the idea that "like goes with like"—if something seems similar to a prototype, we assume it belongs to that category or will behave similarly.

Example

Imagine reading a description of "Linda": she's deeply concerned with social justice and studied philosophy. When asked whether she's more likely to be (a) a bank teller or (b) a bank teller and active in the feminist movement, most people choose (b), despite it being statistically less probable. This is the **conjunction fallacy**, driven by the representativeness heuristic. Linda fits the stereotype of a feminist, so people are more likely to match her with that group—even if it defies logic.

Why It Works

The heuristic works because the human brain seeks patterns and categories to process vast information efficiently. In everyday life, resemblance often correlates with category membership or outcomes. For example, if something looks poisonous (e.g., bright frogs), it often is. Using resemblance as a cue has survival value in many real-world settings. However, it becomes problematic when statistical reasoning is required, especially in domains involving randomness, base rates, or probabilities.

How It Works

This heuristic functions by comparing new information to mental prototypes or stereotypes. When encountering a person or event, the brain:

1. **Identifies a prototype** (e.g., what a typical doctor, criminal, or artist looks like).

2. **Matches features** of the new case to that prototype.

3. **Infers likelihood or outcome** based on the degree of resemblance—often ignoring actual probabilities or prior distributions (base rates).

This shortcut leads to common errors such as base rate neglect, insensitivity to sample size, and misconceptions about randomness.

Application

In **hiring decisions**, managers may prefer candidates who "look the part" (e.g., confident, assertive) based on stereotypes of successful employees, rather than objective qualifications. Similarly, in **medical diagnosis**, doctors might misdiagnose rare diseases if a patient's symptoms strongly match a prototypical case, neglecting base rate frequencies.

Key Insights

- It simplifies decision-making but can systematically distort judgment.

- People tend to ignore base rates and actual statistical distributions.

- It's especially misleading when randomness is involved (e.g., gambling fallacies).

- Being aware of this heuristic can improve rational decision-making in fields like law, investing, and science.

In essence, while the representativeness heuristic enables quick judgments, it often leads to flawed conclusions when resemblance substitutes for reality.

3. Anchoring and adjustment heuristic

The *anchoring and adjustment heuristic* is a cognitive shortcut where individuals begin with an initial reference point (the "anchor") and make adjustments to reach an estimate or decision. First described by **Tversky and Kahneman (1974)**, this heuristic shows that people often rely too heavily on the anchor—even when it's arbitrary or unrelated—and adjust insufficiently from it.

Example

In a classic experiment, participants spun a wheel rigged to land on either 10 or 65. Then they were asked whether the percentage of African countries in the United Nations was higher or lower than that number, followed by their own estimate. Those who saw 10 gave much lower estimates than those who saw 65, even though the anchor (the wheel) was meaningless. This shows how anchoring can powerfully distort judgment.

Why It Works

The heuristic works because people use available information as a starting point when making decisions under uncertainty. When precise knowledge is lacking, even irrelevant or random numbers can influence final judgments. The brain clings to the first number as a foothold, adjusting from there but not enough. This is partly due to cognitive laziness (conserving mental effort) and partly because we implicitly treat the anchor as informative, even when it isn't.

How It Works

Anchoring and adjustment occur in two stages:

1. **Anchor Activation**: A numerical value (either externally provided or self-generated) is introduced. This value "primes" the brain and becomes the initial basis for judgment.

2. **Insufficient Adjustment**: The person adjusts away from the anchor to reach a final estimate, but usually not enough, especially under time pressure or uncertainty.

This process is automatic and hard to override, even when the anchor is known to be irrelevant.

Application

In **negotiation**, anchoring is a powerful tool. A seller might set an initial high price to anchor the buyer's expectations. Even if the final sale price is much lower, it is typically higher than if a lower initial offer had been made. Similarly, in **court sentencing**, judges' decisions can be influenced by initial sentencing suggestions— even arbitrary ones.

Key Insights

- Anchoring is pervasive across domains: pricing, forecasting, valuation, negotiation, and risk assessment.

- Even irrelevant anchors can skew rational judgment.

- The effect is stronger when people are uncertain or uninformed.

- Training in critical thinking or awareness of anchoring can help mitigate its influence—but rarely eliminate it.

In essence, anchoring illustrates how our minds are tethered to initial information, often without realizing its grip.

4. Recognition heuristic

The *recognition heuristic* is a cognitive rule of thumb that suggests when people are faced with a decision between two objects, and only one is recognized, they will infer that the recognized object has the higher value on a particular criterion. This heuristic was formally introduced by **Goldstein and Gigerenzer (1999)** as part of the broader framework of *fast and frugal heuristics*.

It operates under the assumption that *recognition correlates with relevance or importance*. In uncertain environments, especially where people lack detailed knowledge, recognition acts as a useful cue for making decisions quickly and with minimal information processing.

Example

Imagine you're asked: "Which city has a larger population—San Diego or San Antonio?" If you recognize "San Diego" but not "San Antonio," the recognition heuristic suggests you'll infer that San Diego is larger. Surprisingly, this often leads to correct answers, especially in domains where recognition genuinely reflects real-world prevalence or significance (e.g., cities, sports teams, brands).

In experiments, German students correctly guessed that "San Diego" had a larger population than "San Antonio" more often than American students—because fewer Germans had heard of

San Antonio, so they leaned on recognition, while Americans tried to use more detailed (and sometimes incorrect) knowledge.

Why It Works

It works because, in many environments, *recognition is correlated with frequency, size, quality, or success*. Well-known cities tend to be larger, recognized athletes are often more successful, and familiar brands usually have higher market shares. The brain leverages this ecological correlation to make fast, reasonably accurate judgments.

Additionally, the heuristic conserves cognitive effort. Instead of evaluating many variables or making complex comparisons, the mind uses a simple "recognition = value" logic. In many real-world scenarios, this leads to correct decisions with minimal cognitive cost.

How It Works

The recognition heuristic is used when:

1. **One option is recognized** and the other is not.

2. **The goal is to infer a value or rank** (e.g., size, performance, popularity).

3. **Recognition is linked to the criterion** (i.e., the decision context must be one where recognition is a valid cue).

Importantly, it's not used when both options are recognized or when recognition is irrelevant to the goal.

Application

In **marketing**, the recognition heuristic is vital. Consumers often choose familiar brands over unfamiliar ones, even without comparing features. This is why companies invest heavily in brand awareness. In **finance**, investors might favour well-known stocks (e.g., Apple or Amazon) over unfamiliar ones, assuming they are more stable or profitable.

Key Insights

- Recognition is not knowledge; it's a cue, not a conclusion.
- The heuristic is adaptive when recognition aligns with the decision criterion.
- Over-reliance can be problematic if recognition is driven by bias (e.g., media hype).
- It outperforms more complex strategies in certain conditions, especially under uncertainty and limited knowledge.

Ultimately, the recognition heuristic exemplifies how humans exploit structure in their environment to make fast, effective decisions with little information.

5. Fluency heuristic

The *fluency heuristic* is a mental shortcut where, between two alternatives, people are more likely to choose the one that is processed more easily or fluently. This heuristic is based on the idea that the *ease with which information is retrieved or processed* can be an indicator of value, truth, or frequency. It is a refinement of the recognition heuristic and is rooted in the broader theory of *ecological rationality*—the notion that humans use environmental cues to make fast, efficient decisions.

Coined and studied by psychologists such as **Hertwig, Schooler, and Goldstein**, the fluency heuristic suggests that, all else being equal, smoother mental processing influences judgment, especially under uncertainty or time pressure.

Example

Suppose you are asked: "Which brand of batteries lasts longer— Duracell or an unfamiliar-sounding brand like 'Energoplus'?" Even if you have no concrete information, you might infer that Duracell is better. Why? The name "Duracell" is more familiar and easier to process, which gives it a cognitive advantage. This fluency of recognition and pronunciation nudges you toward perceiving it as more reliable or superior.

Similarly, in experiments, stocks with easily pronounceable ticker symbols (e.g., "KAR" vs. "RDO") are often judged as better investments, and in some cases, even yield higher short-term returns due to increased investor confidence.

Why It Works

The fluency heuristic works because in many environments, fluency *correlates* with meaningful attributes. Things we've encountered more often or processed more frequently tend to be more relevant, trustworthy, or popular. Fluency also saves cognitive effort: if one item "feels" easier, it is mentally processed as more favourable without requiring analysis.

Moreover, our brains have evolved to associate processing ease with safety, truth, and familiarity—a phenomenon seen in effects like the *illusion of truth*, where repeated statements are more likely to be believed.

How It Works

The fluency heuristic activates when:

1. Two or more options are evaluated.
2. One option is processed more fluently (e.g., it's more readable, familiar, or easier to pronounce).
3. The decision goal is value-based (e.g., choosing what's better, safer, or more trustworthy).
4. Other information is scarce or complex.

The mind uses fluency as a tiebreaker or primary cue when deeper analysis is unavailable or cognitively costly.

Application

In **branding and design**, companies use the fluency heuristic to their advantage by choosing simple, memorable names, clean fonts, and easy-to-read packaging. In **legal or political communication**, messages that are linguistically simpler or repeated often are more likely to be accepted or remembered by the public.

Key Insights

- Fluency is not accuracy, but it *feels* reliable.

- It highlights how cognitive ease influences belief and choice.

- Overuse can lead to biases—fluent items are not always better.

- It's particularly powerful in fast, low-information decisions.

Ultimately, the fluency heuristic reveals how subtle features of how we process information—not just what we know—shape our judgments and preferences.

6. Affect heuristic

The *affect heuristic* is a mental shortcut in which people rely on their emotional responses—*affect*—to make decisions quickly and efficiently. Rather than analytically weighing pros and cons, individuals use how they *feel* about a situation, person, or object as a guide to judgment. This heuristic was explored in depth by **Slovic, Finucane, Peters, and MacGregor (2002)**, who showed that affect acts as a "compass" for rapid decision-making under uncertainty.

In this model, affect is not just emotion in a vague sense—it's a fast, automatic, and often unconscious gut feeling, which can dominate our evaluations of risk and benefit, even when facts suggest otherwise.

Example

Imagine being asked whether nuclear energy is safe. If your immediate emotional response to the word "nuclear" is fear or anxiety—perhaps shaped by media images of disasters like Chernobyl—you're more likely to judge it as risky, even if you have no technical understanding of how nuclear reactors work. Conversely, if someone feels positively about "green energy" and innovation, they might rate nuclear power as low-risk and high-benefit.

Studies show that when people perceive an activity or product as high in benefit (e.g., vaccinations, flying), they simultaneously rate its risks as low—*and vice versa*. This inverse relationship, driven by affect, often overrides objective risk-benefit analysis.

Why It Works

The affect heuristic works because emotions are evolutionarily tuned to help us make rapid decisions in complex, uncertain environments. Emotions condense large amounts of information into a single, intuitive feeling, which saves cognitive effort. Our ancestors needed to react quickly to threats or rewards—hesitating to analyse a predator could be fatal. Today, this same system guides decisions ranging from what we eat to how we vote.

How It Works

1. **Stimulus Encounter**: A person is exposed to a stimulus (e.g., word, image, scenario).

2. **Affective Reaction**: An immediate positive or negative emotional response arises.

3. **Judgment Shortcut**: Instead of evaluating facts, the person uses this emotional "tag" to infer risks, benefits, or preferences.

4. **Bias Reinforcement**: Because these feelings feel like rational conclusions, people rarely question them.

This heuristic is often implicit and influences choices even when individuals believe they are being logical.

Application

In **public policy and health communication**, the affect heuristic is vital. Anti-smoking campaigns, for example, use disturbing imagery to provoke negative affect, making smoking seem riskier. In contrast, pro-environmental campaigns use calming or uplifting imagery to increase positive affect and encourage green behaviours. Similarly, marketers aim to create brand experiences that "feel good," relying on emotional connection more than detailed features.

Key Insights

- Affect acts faster than reasoning and can override analytical thinking.

- People's judgments of risk and benefit often reflect how they *feel*, not what they *know*.

- It can be manipulated through framing, imagery, and emotional appeals.

- Recognizing its influence can lead to more balanced, reflective decisions.

In sum, the affect heuristic shows that feelings are not just noise in decision-making—they are often the main signal.

7. Take-the-best heuristic

The *Take-the-Best* heuristic is a simple, fast decision-making strategy that relies on the most predictive piece of information—called a "cue"—to make a choice between two alternatives. Rather than weighing all available information, the decision-maker searches through cues in order of validity and chooses based on the first cue that discriminates between options. This heuristic was developed by **Gigerenzer and Goldstein (1996)** within the *fast and frugal heuristics* framework, which emphasizes how humans make adaptive decisions under constraints like time, uncertainty, or limited knowledge.

This strategy contradicts traditional rational models that assume more information and computation lead to better decisions. Instead, Take-the-Best suggests that *less* information, intelligently used, can be more effective.

Example

Imagine you're asked to decide which of two cities—Düsseldorf or Stuttgart—has a larger population. You have limited knowledge, but you do know that Stuttgart has a professional football team and Düsseldorf does not. If team presence is your most valid cue (historically associated with city size), you'll choose Stuttgart based solely on that cue and ignore others. You won't factor in economic data, tourism stats, or geographic size—just the first cue that "takes the best" shot at the answer.

Why It Works

Take-the-Best works because in many real-world environments, information is redundant, and not all cues are equally valuable. Some cues strongly predict outcomes, while others add little or even noise. By focusing only on the most predictive cue, the heuristic avoids overfitting, reduces cognitive load, and is less vulnerable to irrelevant data. It's especially effective when time is limited or information is incomplete.

Research has shown that in some domains, Take-the-Best performs as well as or better than complex statistical models— particularly when the environment has a clear cue hierarchy and uncertainty is high.

How It Works

1. **Cue Ordering**: Cues (predictors) are ranked by validity— how well they predict the outcome.

2. **Search Process**: The decision-maker scans cues in order of validity.

3. **Stopping Rule**: As soon as a cue discriminates between the options (applies to one but not the other), the search stops.

4. **Decision Rule**: The alternative favoured by the first discriminating cue is chosen.

Importantly, the process ignores all remaining information once a cue decides the outcome.

Application

In **medical diagnosis**, Take-the-Best can be used by physicians who rely on one key symptom to rule in or out a condition—such as chest pain radiating to the left arm as a key cue for a heart attack. In **consumer choice**, buyers might decide between smartphones based only on brand reputation, ignoring specifications if brand is their top cue.

Key Insights

- Efficiency: It balances speed with accuracy using minimal information.

- Ecological Rationality: It works best in environments where cue validity is uneven.

- Robustness: It's less prone to error from overanalysing or irrelevant data.

- Limitations: It can underperform when cues are of equal or uncertain value.

The Take-the-Best heuristic demonstrates that sometimes, knowing *just enough* beats knowing *everything*.

8. Default heuristic

The *default heuristic* is a cognitive shortcut where individuals tend to stick with a pre-set option—*the default*—rather than actively selecting an alternative. This heuristic assumes that the default option is the recommended, most natural, or least effortful choice, and thus likely to be the best or most appropriate. It reflects a broader principle in decision-making: *people often opt for the path of least resistance*.

Rooted in behavioural economics and decision science, the default heuristic has been widely studied by researchers like **Richard Thaler** and **Cass Sunstein**, especially in the context of "nudge theory." It highlights how the *structure of choices* can significantly influence behaviour, even without changing the options themselves.

Example

Consider organ donation policies. Countries with *opt-in* systems (where citizens must actively register to become donors) have significantly lower donor rates than countries with *opt-out* systems (where all citizens are presumed donors unless they choose otherwise). For instance, Austria, with an opt-out default, has a donor rate above 90%, while neighbouring Germany, with opt-in, has rates closer to 12%. The default heuristic explains this stark contrast: most people accept the default, regardless of their actual preferences.

Why It Works

The default heuristic works for several reasons:

- **Cognitive Effort**: Changing the default requires action and thought. Many people avoid that effort.

- **Perceived Endorsement**: Defaults are often interpreted as recommendations by authorities or experts.

- **Loss Aversion**: Switching from a default can feel like giving something up, triggering resistance.

- **Decision Paralysis**: When people are uncertain or overwhelmed, they tend to stick with the status quo.

These forces combine to make defaults especially influential in high-stakes, complex, or unfamiliar decisions—exactly when thoughtful deliberation would ideally occur.

How It Works

1. **Choice Environment**: A decision is presented with one option pre-selected or automatically applied.

2. **Passive Acceptance**: Most individuals fail to change the default due to effort, trust, or inertia.

3. **Outcome**: The default option ends up shaping behaviour more than personal preference or analysis.

This process typically operates subconsciously, especially when users are unaware that a default is influencing them.

Application

In **retirement savings plans**, employers who auto-enrol employees with a default contribution rate see much higher participation than those requiring employees to opt in. In **software settings**, most users stick with default configurations— be it privacy settings, font types, or language preferences.

Public policymakers and designers use default settings to nudge individuals toward socially beneficial choices—like greener energy plans or automatic renewals for safety subscriptions— without removing freedom of choice.

Key Insights

- Defaults are powerful levers of behaviour because they capitalize on human inertia.

- People often infer social or expert approval from defaults.

- The effect is strongest when individuals are busy, uncertain, or indifferent.

- Ethically, defaults should be used transparently and in the public interest.

Ultimately, the default heuristic shows how seemingly small design choices can have massive impacts on decisions and societal outcomes.

9. Simulation heuristic

The *simulation heuristic* is a mental shortcut where people assess the likelihood or emotional impact of an event based on how easily they can imagine or mentally simulate it. Proposed by psychologists **Kahneman and Tversky (1982)**, this heuristic plays a major role in how individuals make sense of outcomes, especially unexpected ones, and how they assign causality or regret.

Rather than relying on statistics or data, the mind substitutes a complex judgment (e.g., "How likely was this to happen?") with the ease of constructing a plausible narrative or alternate scenario ("Can I easily imagine this happening or not happening?"). The easier it is to simulate, the more likely or emotionally significant it feels.

Example

Imagine two passengers miss a flight. One arrives at the airport 30 minutes late, while the other misses it by just two minutes. Objectively, both missed the flight. But people typically feel much more sympathy or frustration for the second person. Why? Because it's easier to mentally simulate alternative scenarios in which they *just* made it—"If only the taxi hadn't hit traffic," or "If they'd skipped the coffee stop." The ease of imagining a different outcome fuels greater emotional response and perceived misfortune.

Why It Works

The simulation heuristic works because the human brain is wired to understand the world through stories and cause-effect relationships. Mental simulations help us predict outcomes, assign responsibility, and process emotions. This heuristic is efficient for quick evaluations of "what could have been," guiding responses like blame, regret, or relief.

It also taps into *counterfactual thinking*, the mental construction of alternatives to past events. These imagined scenarios influence not just how we understand events, but how we *feel* about them.

How It Works

1. **Trigger Event**: An outcome—usually surprising, emotional, or close to a boundary—is experienced.

2. **Mental Simulation**: The mind quickly constructs alternative versions of the outcome (what could have gone differently).

3. **Emotional or Causal Judgment**: The ease of these simulations influences perceptions of likelihood, fairness, blame, or regret.

The heuristic often overrides logical analysis. Events that are harder to imagine (due to complexity or unfamiliarity) feel less likely, even if they're more probable statistically.

Application

In **legal settings**, the simulation heuristic can affect jury decisions. Jurors may more easily simulate a defendant acting differently in a highly emotional case, which can influence verdicts or sentencing. In **marketing**, advertisers create vivid "what if" scenarios to help consumers imagine the benefits of using a product—or the regret of not using it.

In **health messaging**, showing how easily one could have avoided illness (e.g., "If only they'd gotten the vaccine...") activates simulation and increases the perceived need for action.

Key Insights

- Emotional impact increases with the ease of imagining alternatives.

- The heuristic drives blame, regret, and moral judgment, not just probability estimates.

- It explains why near-misses or "almost" events feel especially intense.

- Understanding it can improve resilience, empathy, and communication strategies.

In essence, the simulation heuristic shows how the mind turns imagination into perceived reality.

10. Familiarity heuristic

The *familiarity heuristic* is a mental shortcut where individuals judge the likelihood, value, or safety of something based on how familiar it feels. In essence, people are more likely to prefer or trust things they recognize or have encountered before, even if they lack detailed knowledge about them. This heuristic simplifies decision-making by allowing familiarity to serve as a stand-in for reliability or correctness.

It's closely related to the recognition and fluency heuristics but places emphasis on *previous exposure* and subjective comfort rather than ease of processing or mere recognition. Familiarity is a deeply rooted cue in human cognition, tied to emotion, memory, and survival.

Example

Imagine someone is choosing between two vacation destinations: one is a well-known city they've heard about often (like Paris), while the other is a lesser-known, though perhaps more affordable and equally beautiful town. Even if they know little about either, they're more likely to choose Paris simply because it feels familiar. This sense of knowing, even without detail, creates a sense of safety and positive expectation.

This is why tourists often dine at recognizable international fast-food chains when traveling—familiarity provides comfort and a reduced sense of risk, even in unfamiliar environments.

Why It Works

The familiarity heuristic works because the brain associates repeated exposure with safety and trust. Evolutionarily, familiar things were often safer—foods, environments, people—and unfamiliar things carried unknown risks. This adaptive bias toward the known persists today and influences modern decisions, from whom to trust to what products to buy.

Repeated exposure also leads to the *mere exposure effect*—a psychological phenomenon where people develop a preference for things simply because they are familiar with them. Familiarity often generates positive affect, reducing uncertainty and cognitive load.

How It Works

1. **Exposure**: The individual has previously encountered the person, place, idea, or object.

2. **Judgment**: When faced with a decision, the familiar option feels more comfortable or trustworthy.

3. **Selection**: The individual chooses or favors the familiar over the unfamiliar, even if the unfamiliar is objectively better.

This process is often automatic and emotionally driven, bypassing deliberate analysis or fact-checking.

Application

In **marketing**, companies rely heavily on the familiarity heuristic. Repeated advertising, logos, slogans, and jingles all serve to build brand familiarity, increasing consumer trust and preference. In **politics**, candidates with more media exposure often gain voter favour simply due to name recognition, regardless of their policies.

Even in **hiring**, candidates with names, schools, or past companies that feel familiar to the recruiter may be rated more favourably.

Key Insights

- Familiarity increases perceived trust, safety, and value.

- It functions as an emotional comfort mechanism, especially under uncertainty.

- Overreliance can lead to biased decisions or missed opportunities.

- Awareness of this heuristic can help counter unconscious favouritism or habitual choices.

In short, the familiarity heuristic reveals how our preference for the known often shapes our perceptions, choices, and behaviours—whether or not we're aware of it.

⁜ Judgment and Decision-Making Heuristics

11. Elimination by aspects heuristic

Elimination by Aspects

Elimination by aspects (EBA) is a decision-making heuristic introduced by psychologist **Amos Tversky (1972)**. It describes how people make complex choices by sequentially eliminating options that lack certain desirable attributes (or "aspects"). Rather than evaluating all options holistically or comparing them in parallel, individuals focus on one criterion at a time and eliminate alternatives that don't meet it, continuing this process until only one option remains.

This approach simplifies decision-making in situations with many alternatives and limited cognitive resources, reducing the burden of weighing all options simultaneously.

Example

Imagine you're shopping for a new smartphone. You have a list of ten models. First, you eliminate any phone that doesn't have at least 128GB of storage. Next, from the remaining phones, you remove those without 5G capability. Then, you eliminate options over a certain price. Eventually, you're left with just one model that satisfies all your top-tier needs. You didn't compare all ten models on every feature; instead, you eliminated based on critical aspects, one step at a time.

Why It Works

The EBA heuristic works because it mimics how people naturally reduce decision complexity. In real-world settings, evaluating every alternative across every dimension is mentally exhausting and often unnecessary. By focusing on one attribute at a time— typically the most important or salient—people can narrow their options efficiently without engaging in full-scale analysis.

It also reflects how decisions are often shaped by *non-compensatory reasoning*—where a deficit in one key attribute cannot be outweighed by strengths in others. For example, a buyer might instantly reject any home without a garden, regardless of other appealing features.

How It Works

1. **Attribute Ranking**: The decision-maker identifies and ranks aspects (criteria) in order of importance.

2. **Aspect-Based Filtering**: Alternatives that do not meet the minimum requirement for the highest-priority aspect are eliminated.

3. **Iterative Elimination**: The process repeats with the next-most-important aspect, applied to the remaining options.

4. **Final Selection**: This continues until only one option (or a manageable shortlist) remains.

Unlike compensatory models, EBA does not weigh or trade off between features. Once an aspect fails, the option is discarded.

Application

In **consumer behaviour**, EBA is used frequently—whether in choosing appliances, booking flights, or selecting insurance plans. For instance, travellers might first eliminate all flights without direct routes, then those exceeding a budget, and finally pick the earliest departure time.

In **HR and recruitment**, hiring managers may eliminate applicants lacking a required qualification before considering experience, cultural fit, or other secondary factors.

Key Insights

- EBA is efficient, especially in environments with many choices.

- It reflects real-world decision behaviour better than rational utility models.

- It is non-compensatory: missing a key criterion disqualifies an option outright.

- While it reduces complexity, it may overlook better overall options that fail on a single aspect.

Ultimately, Elimination by Aspects is a practical, structured way to narrow decisions when facing complexity and information overload.

12. Satisficing heuristic

Satisficing

Satisficing is a decision-making heuristic where individuals seek a solution or option that is "good enough," rather than the absolute best. The term was coined by **Herbert A. Simon (1956)**, who combined "satisfy" and "suffice" to describe a strategy that balances aspiration with practicality. Simon introduced the concept to challenge the prevailing economic notion of humans as perfectly rational agents who always optimize decisions.

According to the satisficing heuristic, people set minimum acceptable criteria for their choices and select the first option that meets those criteria, even if better options might exist. This is especially common in situations involving limited time, cognitive constraints, or incomplete information.

Example

Imagine you're looking for a new apartment. You define your essential criteria: it must be within 30 minutes of work, under $1,200/month, and have at least one bedroom. You start searching and find a listing that meets all three. Even though it may not be the cheapest or most spacious, you rent it because it satisfies your needs. You don't examine every possible apartment or search indefinitely for the "perfect" one—you satisficed.

Why It Works

Satisficing works because real-world decision-making is often constrained by **bounded rationality**—the idea that human cognition is limited in terms of time, attention, and processing capacity. Trying to find the optimal solution can be unrealistic, costly, or even paralyzing (a phenomenon known as *choice overload*). By setting a threshold and choosing the first option that clears it, individuals conserve cognitive resources and still meet their goals effectively.

Moreover, satisficing reduces the psychological burden of regret and perfectionism. When people aim only to "do well enough," they're less likely to ruminate over missed opportunities.

How It Works

1. **Set Criteria**: The individual defines what counts as "good enough" based on their goals or constraints.

2. **Search**: They sequentially consider available options.

3. **Stop Rule**: The first option that meets or exceeds the defined criteria is selected.

4. **No Further Search**: Once a satisfactory option is found, the process ends—no exhaustive comparison or optimization occurs.

This is a non-exhaustive, aspiration-level strategy rather than a comparative or maximizing one.

Application

In **everyday consumer decisions**, satisficing is common—such as choosing a restaurant, buying clothes, or picking a movie. In **hiring**, employers may select the first qualified candidate who fits the role, rather than continuing to search for a perfect match.

In **emergency response or triage**, where speed matters more than perfection, satisficing allows for quick, effective decisions under pressure.

Key Insights

- Satisficing reflects how people actually make decisions under constraints.

- It avoids the cognitive overload of maximization and supports timely choices.

- While it may miss the "best" outcome, it often leads to satisfactory results with fewer resources.

- Chronic maximizers tend to experience more regret and indecision than satisficers.

Ultimately, satisficing reveals that in a complex world, *"good enough" is often good enough*—and sometimes, it's the smartest path forward.

13. Fast and frugal trees heuristic

Fast and frugal trees (FFTs) are simple, decision-making models that guide choices using a sequential, rule-based structure. Developed by **Gerd Gigerenzer and his colleagues**, FFTs are part of the *fast and frugal heuristics* framework, which proposes that people can make effective decisions with limited time, information, or cognitive effort. These trees rely on a few key cues arranged in a specific order, with clear decision points that allow users to arrive at a conclusion quickly—often more accurately than complex algorithms.

The idea is not to consider all information but to rely on a structured decision path that focuses only on the most predictive cues. This approach challenges the assumption that rational decision-making requires evaluating every available option with statistical precision.

Example

Imagine a hospital emergency room using a fast and frugal tree to decide whether a patient with chest pain should be admitted to the coronary care unit. The tree might include cues such as:

1. Is the electrocardiogram abnormal?
   → If yes, admit.
   → If no, go to next cue.

2. Is the patient experiencing unstable angina?
   → If yes, admit.
   → If no, go to next cue.

3. Is the blood pressure extremely low?
   → If yes, admit.
   → If no, discharge.

Rather than weighing multiple indicators and calculating probabilities, this tree enables a quick and reliable decision with a simple step-by-step path.

Why It Works

FFTs work because they exploit **ecological rationality**—they are tailored to fit real-world environments where decisions are often made under uncertainty and time pressure. These trees reduce cognitive load and minimize the risk of overfitting or information overload. Research has shown that FFTs often perform on par with, or better than, more complex statistical models in domains such as medicine, business, and criminal justice.

They are effective because:

- Only relevant cues are used.

- Irrelevant information is ignored.

- The structure stops information search as soon as a decision is made.

How It Works

1. **Cue Ordering**: Identify the most valid cues and rank them.

2. **Tree Construction**: Build a simple, hierarchical tree where each cue leads to a binary (yes/no) decision.

3. **Sequential Decision**: Progress through the tree until a decision point is reached.

4. **Stopping Rule**: Once a decision is made based on a cue, the process ends—no need to evaluate further.

Application

In **clinical decision-making**, FFTs are used to assess diagnoses rapidly. In **credit scoring**, lenders may use them to approve or reject applicants based on a few key financial indicators. In **legal systems**, parole boards may use FFTs to assess the likelihood of reoffending.

Key Insights

- Simplicity does not equal inaccuracy—FFTs often outperform complex models in real settings.

- FFTs emphasize decision *efficiency* without sacrificing *accuracy*.

- They illustrate that ignoring information can be a strength, not a flaw.

- Well-structured heuristics can match expert judgment while being teachable and transparent.

Fast and frugal trees show that when it comes to decision-making, *less can truly be more*.

14. One-reason decision making heuristic

One-reason decision making is a heuristic strategy where a choice between alternatives is made based on a single, most important cue or reason. Once that cue discriminates between options, the decision is made immediately, and no further information is considered. This approach stems from the broader *fast and frugal heuristics* framework developed by **Gerd Gigerenzer** and colleagues, which argues that under conditions of uncertainty, simple rules often outperform complex calculations.

This heuristic emphasizes **speed and efficiency** over thorough comparison. It assumes that in many real-world environments, one good cue is often sufficient to make an accurate decision, especially when that cue is highly valid or predictive.

Example

Suppose you're choosing between two job applicants. Applicant A has a degree from a top-tier university, while Applicant B does not. If you believe that education pedigree is the most important predictor of job success in this context, and that is your top cue, you select Applicant A—without considering further details like work experience, interview performance, or references. One reason—university ranking—guides the entire decision.

This strategy mirrors how people often make snap judgments in high-pressure situations, relying on a key piece of information that "feels" decisive.

Why It Works

One-reason decision making works because in many environments, cues are not equally informative. Some cues are strongly predictive, while others add little or even noise. Instead of integrating all available information (which is cognitively expensive), this heuristic leverages the most reliable signal.

It also avoids **overfitting**—a problem that occurs when too much irrelevant information is processed. By focusing on just one cue, decision-makers sidestep unnecessary complexity and reduce the chance of distortion caused by weak or misleading data.

How It Works

1. **Cue Identification**: Identify which cue is most valid or important for the specific decision.

2. **Search for Discrimination**: Examine if this cue can differentiate between the options.

3. **Make Decision**: Choose the alternative favoured by this cue.

4. **Stop Rule**: Do not evaluate any additional information once a cue has led to a choice.

This approach assumes that further analysis will not significantly improve the outcome.

Application

In **emergency medicine**, a doctor might use one-reason decision making to quickly decide whether a patient needs to be admitted—for example, if they show a single critical symptom (e.g., crushing chest pain). In **sports scouting**, a coach might select a player based on one outstanding attribute, like sprint speed, if that aligns with the team's specific needs.

Marketers may also apply this heuristic by emphasizing one dominant feature (e.g., "the fastest phone") to drive consumer choice.

Key Insights

- Not all decisions require multiple comparisons—one good reason can be enough.

- It's particularly effective in time-sensitive or high-uncertainty situations.

- Simplicity enhances speed, reduces error, and minimizes decision fatigue.

- This heuristic trades completeness for efficiency—and often wins.

Ultimately, one-reason decision making demonstrates that **less information, well-used, can be more powerful than thorough deliberation**.

15. Escalation of commitment heuristic

The *escalation of commitment* heuristic refers to the tendency of individuals or groups to continue investing time, money, or resources into a failing course of action due to prior investments, even when evidence suggests it would be better to cut losses. This behaviour, often irrational, is driven by a desire to justify past decisions and avoid the emotional cost of failure or loss.

The concept is rooted in behavioural economics and decision theory, notably explored by **Barry Staw (1976)**, and relates closely to the *sunk cost fallacy*. While sunk costs (past investments that cannot be recovered) should not rationally influence future decisions, people often escalate their commitment to avoid admitting failure or to recover losses.

Example

Consider a company that has invested millions into developing a new product. Halfway through, market research reveals that customer interest is low, and competitors are releasing superior alternatives. Despite the warning signs, the leadership team decides to continue the project, pouring more resources into development in hopes that things will turn around. Their reasoning? "We've already come this far." This is classic escalation of commitment—persisting in a losing endeavour to justify prior investments.

Why It Works

Escalation of commitment works—psychologically—because it taps into several powerful biases:

- **Loss aversion**: People feel losses more intensely than gains, making them reluctant to accept previous investments as failures.

- **Cognitive dissonance**: Admitting a poor decision creates psychological discomfort, which people try to resolve by doubling down.

- **Self-justification**: Individuals want to appear consistent and rational, both to themselves and others, so they continue rather than admit error.

- **Social pressure**: In group or organizational contexts, decision-makers may fear judgment for "giving up."

These forces combine to make disengaging feel riskier than continuing, even when evidence suggests otherwise.

How It Works

1. **Initial Decision**: A choice is made, and resources are committed.

2. **Negative Feedback Emerges**: Evidence begins to show the decision may not yield expected outcomes.

3. **Commitment Increases**: Rather than withdrawing, more resources are committed to justify the original decision.

4. **Cycle Repeats**: As the stakes increase, so does the reluctance to abandon the effort.

This cycle often leads to suboptimal outcomes, where good money, time, or energy is thrown after bad.

Application

In **project management**, recognizing escalation of commitment can prevent costly overruns. Teams that regularly reassess projects using objective criteria—ignoring sunk costs—are better positioned to pivot or terminate failing efforts. In **public policy**, governments sometimes persist with ineffective programs due to political or reputational investment.

In **personal life**, people may stay in unhappy relationships or unsuitable careers longer than they should, simply because they've already "put in so much time."

Key Insights

- Escalation is driven by emotion, identity, and loss aversion—not rational analysis.

- Recognizing sunk costs as irrelevant is crucial to avoiding this trap.

- Third-party reviews, accountability systems, and pre-defined exit criteria can help curb escalation.

- Admitting failure is often the wisest—and bravest—choice.

Ultimately, the escalation of commitment heuristic reminds us that **cutting losses is not giving up—it's choosing wisely**.

16. Loss aversion heuristic

Loss aversion is a cognitive bias and heuristic where people tend to prefer avoiding losses rather than acquiring equivalent gains. In simple terms, **losing $100 feels worse than gaining $100 feels good**. This principle was first formally introduced by **Daniel Kahneman and Amos Tversky** in their influential *Prospect Theory* (1979), which revolutionized our understanding of human decision-making under risk.

The loss aversion heuristic suggests that individuals often evaluate outcomes relative to a reference point (often the status quo) and perceive losses more intensely than equivalent gains. As a result, they make decisions that are disproportionately aimed at preventing losses, even when those choices may not be optimal.

Example

Imagine you're given two options:
Option A: A guaranteed gain of $500
Option B: A 50% chance to win $1,000 and a 50% chance to win nothing

Most people choose Option A, preferring a sure gain over a risky one.
Now flip the scenario:
Option C: A guaranteed loss of $500

Option D: A 50% chance to lose $1,000 and a 50% chance to lose nothing

Here, many people choose Option D—even though it's riskier—just to avoid a guaranteed loss. This reversal in risk preference highlights the power of loss aversion.

Why It Works

Loss aversion works because, from an evolutionary standpoint, losses often posed greater threats to survival than equivalent gains offered benefits. For instance, losing food, shelter, or social status could be life-threatening, whereas gains, while beneficial, were rarely urgent.

Psychologically, losses trigger stronger emotional reactions—like fear, anxiety, and regret—compared to the satisfaction associated with gains. This emotional asymmetry drives the heuristic: to avoid the psychological pain of losing, people act more conservatively or irrationally.

How It Works

1. **Reference Point Established**: Individuals evaluate outcomes relative to a baseline (e.g., current wealth, expectations).

2. **Loss Identified**: Any potential outcome below this point is perceived as a loss.

3. **Avoidance Behaviour**: Decisions are skewed toward avoiding perceived losses, even at the expense of potential gains.

4. **Emotional Influence**: The fear of loss dominates the decision process, often leading to overly cautious or risk-seeking behaviour (depending on framing).

Application

In **marketing**, companies exploit loss aversion by using phrases like "Don't miss out" or "Only a few left"—emphasizing potential loss rather than gain. In **finance**, investors often hold onto losing stocks too long to avoid realizing a loss, even when selling would be more rational.

In **policy-making**, loss aversion explains resistance to change—people often oppose reforms not because they dislike them, but because they fear losing what they currently have.

Key Insights

- People fear losses more than they value equivalent gains.

- Loss aversion can lead to both **overly conservative** and **irrational risk-seeking** behaviour depending on framing.

- Understanding this bias is crucial in economics, leadership, negotiation, and personal finance.

- Framing matters: presenting the same outcome as a loss or gain dramatically changes behaviour.

In essence, the loss aversion heuristic teaches us that **the pain of loss can powerfully shape choices—even more than the promise of reward**.

17. Framing heuristic

The *framing heuristic* refers to a cognitive bias where the way information is presented—or *framed*—significantly influences decision-making, even when the underlying facts remain the same. Introduced and popularized by **Daniel Kahneman and Amos Tversky** as part of *Prospect Theory* (1979), this heuristic reveals that people don't always evaluate options based purely on objective outcomes; instead, they are swayed by the *context* and *language* in which choices are described.

Framing can dramatically alter perception of risk, value, and morality by emphasizing either potential gains or potential losses. This heuristic shows that the same decision can lead to opposite choices depending on how it is worded.

Example

Imagine two treatment options for a disease:

- **Option A** is framed as "saving 200 of 600 people."
- **Option B** is framed as "400 people will die."

Most people choose Option A, even though both describe the same outcome. The positive framing of "lives saved" feels more reassuring than the negative framing of "lives lost."

In a different group, if both options are framed in terms of deaths (e.g., "400 will die" vs. "a one-third chance no one dies and two-thirds chance all die"), the majority may choose the riskier option. This shift illustrates how the framing heuristic overrides logical equivalence.

Why It Works

The framing heuristic works because human decision-making is heavily influenced by **emotions**, **mental shortcuts**, and **reference points**. People are naturally loss-averse, so they react more strongly to the possibility of loss than to gain. A frame that highlights losses triggers more fear, leading to risk-seeking behaviour, while a gain frame encourages caution and risk aversion.

Additionally, people rely on *surface cues* when processing information quickly, and linguistic framing acts as one of those cues.

How It Works

1. **Information Presented**: A choice is described in a specific frame—either positively (gains) or negatively (losses).

2. **Emotional Reaction**: The frame activates a corresponding emotional and cognitive response (hope, fear, caution, urgency).

3. **Decision Bias**: This emotional cue influences preferences, leading to different choices despite equivalent outcomes.

The heuristic tends to operate subconsciously, influencing people even when they believe they're being objective.

Application

In **health communication**, how doctors frame treatment outcomes can affect patients' choices. Saying "90% survival rate" feels more encouraging than "10% mortality rate." In **marketing**, businesses frame discounts as "you save $20" instead of "this item costs $80," triggering a more positive reaction. In **politics**, the framing of policies as "protecting jobs" versus "reducing inefficiency" can sway public support.

Key Insights

- Framing alters decision outcomes without changing actual facts.

- Gain frames encourage risk aversion; loss frames promote risk-taking.

- The heuristic highlights the importance of communication and context.

- Being aware of framing can reduce manipulation and improve decision quality.

Ultimately, the framing heuristic reminds us that **how we say something can be just as influential as what we say**.

18. Status quo heuristic

The *status quo heuristic* refers to the cognitive bias where individuals prefer to maintain their current situation or previous decisions rather than change—even when superior alternatives exist. This mental shortcut simplifies decision-making by defaulting to existing conditions, assuming that what already exists is safer, better, or more appropriate.

This heuristic is closely tied to **loss aversion**, **regret avoidance**, and **decision inertia**, and has been extensively studied in behavioural economics by researchers such as **Samuelson and Zeckhauser (1988)**. It reveals how people value stability and resist change, even when evidence suggests that change would be beneficial.

Example

Imagine an employee has been using a particular software for years. A new software is introduced that is more efficient, user-friendly, and cost-effective. However, the employee continues to use the old system simply because they're familiar with it and don't want to deal with the hassle of learning something new. Even though the switch would improve productivity, the current state feels more comfortable and less risky—demonstrating the pull of the status quo heuristic.

Similarly, when employees are automatically enrolled into retirement savings plans (the status quo), most stick with the default contribution rate and investment strategy—even when better options are available.

Why It Works

The status quo heuristic works because the brain tends to **minimize effort**, **avoid uncertainty**, and **reduce emotional discomfort** associated with potential loss or regret. Maintaining the current state feels psychologically safe and requires no new action, minimizing the fear of making a bad or regrettable decision.

Additionally, people often equate the current state with a social or institutional endorsement—"If this is how it's been, it must be right"—leading to passive acceptance. The fear of making a change that leads to worse outcomes can outweigh the potential benefits of improvement.

How It Works

1. **Decision Context**: A choice involves keeping the current situation or selecting an alternative.

2. **Comparison Bias**: The existing state is evaluated more favourably or less critically than new options.

3. **Inaction Preference**: Individuals choose not to act, sticking with what they already know or have.

4. **Justification**: Rationalizations are made to support the default, often unconsciously.

This process often bypasses objective comparison and reinforces habits, even in dynamic environments.

Application

In **product marketing**, businesses exploit this heuristic by making their products the default option (e.g., pre-checked boxes during checkout). In **public policy**, governments improve outcomes by setting beneficial defaults—such as automatic organ donation enrolment or green energy plans—knowing most people will stick with the status quo.

In **investing**, individuals often hold underperforming assets because selling would require breaking from the status quo, even when switching could lead to better returns.

Key Insights

- The heuristic reduces cognitive and emotional costs but can hinder innovation and improvement.

- Defaults have a powerful influence on behaviour, even without coercion.

- Awareness of the status quo bias can promote more intentional and flexible decision-making.

- Proactively questioning the default can unlock better options.

Ultimately, the status quo heuristic shows that **sometimes, the biggest barrier to change isn't complexity—it's comfort.**

19. Equity heuristic

The *equity heuristic* is a mental shortcut where individuals make decisions based on perceived fairness or equal distribution, rather than maximizing outcomes or evaluating all available information. It reflects a strong human tendency to favour equality—often opting to divide resources, rewards, or responsibilities evenly, regardless of merit, efficiency, or context.

This heuristic is especially common in social, moral, and cooperative contexts. It allows people to simplify complex decisions by applying a straightforward fairness rule: "everyone should get the same" or "contributions should be matched by rewards." While this can promote harmony and reduce conflict, it can also lead to suboptimal outcomes when equal treatment doesn't reflect actual needs or efforts.

Example

Imagine a manager has a $10,000 bonus pool to divide among four team members. Two team members worked significantly harder and contributed more, while the others had average performance. Instead of evaluating performance metrics in detail, the manager divides the bonus equally—$2,500 each—so no one feels left out or treated unfairly. This is the equity heuristic in action: simplicity and perceived fairness override detailed evaluation.

Alternatively, in group projects, people often expect equal credit or equal grading, even if not all participants contributed equally.

Why It Works

The equity heuristic works because it reduces **social friction**, **cognitive effort**, and the **emotional burden** of evaluating others. Human beings are wired for fairness—evolutionarily, fairness helped maintain cooperation and trust in small groups. Violating fairness norms often leads to resentment, conflict, or even punishment, which makes equal distribution a safe and socially acceptable choice.

Moreover, fairness is deeply tied to emotional and moral reasoning. Choosing equal outcomes provides psychological comfort and avoids accusations of bias or favouritism.

How It Works

1. **Decision Context**: A resource, task, or reward needs to be distributed among individuals.

2. **Simplification**: Rather than assess merit, contribution, or utility, the decision-maker applies a fairness rule.

3. **Equal Distribution**: Resources are divided equally or in proportion to easily observed factors (e.g., time worked, number of tasks).

4. **Emotional Reinforcement**: The outcome "feels right" because it aligns with fairness expectations, reducing potential backlash.

This heuristic bypasses nuanced evaluation in favour of social acceptability and ease.

Application

In **education**, teachers may award equal participation grades even when students contributed unequally. In **family dynamics**, parents often try to give children equal gifts or attention to avoid feelings of favouritism. In **workplaces**, leaders may distribute workloads or benefits evenly to maintain morale and cohesion.

Even in **international relations**, aid is sometimes distributed evenly across regions to avoid political tension, rather than targeting areas with greatest need.

Key Insights

- Equity promotes social stability but may sacrifice efficiency or merit-based outcomes.

- It reflects emotional reasoning—what "feels fair" over what is strictly rational.

- The heuristic is especially powerful in group dynamics, where harmony is valued.

- Recognizing when equity overrides better judgment can help balance fairness with effectiveness.

Ultimately, the equity heuristic shows that **in human decision-making, perceived fairness often trumps pure logic**—for better or worse.

20. Mental accounting heuristic

Mental accounting is a cognitive heuristic and behavioural economics concept that describes how people mentally categorize and treat money differently depending on its source, intended use, or form, even though money is fungible. The term was introduced by **Richard Thaler (1980)**, a Nobel Prize-winning economist, who showed that individuals do not treat all dollars equally—violating classical economic theory, which assumes that money has uniform value regardless of context.

Instead of viewing money as part of a single pool, people create mental "accounts"—such as savings, entertainment, rent, or windfalls—and make spending and saving decisions based on these artificial categories. These mental divisions affect behaviour in powerful, often irrational ways.

Example

Suppose someone receives a $1,000 tax refund. They mentally label it as a *bonus* or *extra money* and decide to splurge on a vacation. Yet, they have $3,000 in credit card debt with a 20% interest rate. From a rational standpoint, the best use of the $1,000 is to pay down the high-interest debt. However, because the refund is placed in a different "mental account" (a gain rather than an obligation), it's treated differently.

Similarly, people may be more willing to spend cash won in a lottery or casino than money earned through hard work, even though the money is identical in value.

Why It Works

Mental accounting works because it simplifies complex financial decisions. By breaking down money into categories, people can manage budgets more easily and make spending feel more purposeful. Emotion also plays a key role—labelling money influences the feelings attached to spending or saving it. "Fun money" feels easier to spend than "retirement savings," even if both come from the same bank account.

It also provides a sense of control, especially in uncertain or overwhelming financial situations. Mental categories reduce the cognitive load required to make each decision anew.

How It Works

1. **Categorization**: Individuals mentally assign money to categories based on source (e.g., salary, gift), purpose (e.g., rent, entertainment), or context (e.g., regular income vs. windfall).

2. **Rule Application**: They apply different rules for spending, saving, or risk-taking depending on the account.

3. **Behavioural Outcome**: These distinctions drive decisions, even when they contradict financial logic (e.g., spending a gift rather than saving it).

These accounts are internal, often subconscious, and can override economic rationality.

Application

In **personal finance**, mental accounting influences how people budget, save, and spend. Financial advisors use it to help clients allocate money into labelled sub-accounts—like emergency funds or travel savings—which improves discipline. In **marketing**, retailers may offer "store credit" rather than cash refunds, knowing customers treat it differently and are more likely to spend it impulsively.

Governments also use mental accounting in **policy framing**, such as "gas taxes" being earmarked for road maintenance—creating a perceived fairness in spending.

Key Insights

- People assign subjective value to money based on mental categories.

- This helps with budgeting but can lead to irrational decisions.

- Mental accounting explains behaviours like splurging with windfalls or over-saving in some areas while overspending in others.

- Awareness of this heuristic can improve financial decision-making by encouraging holistic thinking.

Ultimately, *mental accounting* shows that **how we *think* about money often matters more than the money itself.**

AI and Computer Science Heuristics

21. A* search heuristic

The *A** search heuristic is a powerful algorithm used in computer science and artificial intelligence for finding the most efficient path between two points. It is widely used in pathfinding and graph traversal problems, such as navigation systems, game AI, and robotics. A* combines the strengths of both **uniform-cost search** (which explores paths with the lowest cumulative cost) and **greedy best-first search** (which prioritizes paths that appear closest to the goal).

Introduced by **Peter Hart, Nils Nilsson, and Bertram Raphael (1968)**, the A* algorithm uses both actual cost from the start (denoted *g(n)*) and an estimated cost to the goal (denoted *h(n)*) to determine which node to explore next. The sum of these—*f(n)* = *g(n)* + *h(n)*—guides the search.

Example

Imagine a GPS navigation system calculating the best driving route from Point A to Point B. The system doesn't just look at distance—it considers traffic, road conditions, and estimated travel time. A* search uses this information to evaluate multiple routes, calculating both the distance travelled so far (*g*) and an estimate of the remaining distance to the destination (*h*), choosing the path with the lowest combined value of *f(n)*.

So, rather than just heading in the general direction of the goal (like a greedy algorithm might) or only choosing the cheapest step-by-step path (like Dijkstra's algorithm), A* smartly balances *where you've been* and *how far you still have to go*.

Why It Works

A* search works effectively because it uses a heuristic to make informed guesses about the best path, dramatically reducing the number of nodes it needs to explore compared to blind or brute-force methods. When the heuristic function $h(n)$ is **admissible** (never overestimates the actual cost), A* is guaranteed to find the optimal solution. When it's also **consistent** (monotonic), the algorithm becomes even more efficient.

Its efficiency stems from its ability to zero in on the goal while avoiding paths that are unlikely to succeed, blending exploration and exploitation in an optimal way.

How It Works

1. **Initialization**: Begin at the starting node, calculating $f(n) = g(n) + h(n)$.

2. **Node Selection**: From a priority queue, select the node with the lowest $f(n)$ value.

3. **Expansion**: Explore that node's neighbours, updating g, h, and f values.

4. **Repeat**: Continue until the goal node is selected from the queue.

5. **Path Reconstruction**: Trace the path back from goal to start using stored predecessor information.

Application

In **video games**, A* is used for character movement, enabling NPCs (non-player characters) to navigate complex environments. In **robotics**, it helps robots plan routes through dynamic or obstacle-filled spaces. In **network routing**, A* assists in optimizing data packet delivery. It's also used in **logistics** and **airline route planning**, where finding cost-effective paths is critical.

Key Insights

- A* search is efficient, optimal, and widely applicable when the heuristic is well-designed.

- It bridges logic-based and heuristic-based search, making it versatile in real-time systems.

- Its performance depends heavily on the accuracy and admissibility of the heuristic function.

- A* is foundational in AI and has inspired many advanced variants and optimizations.

Ultimately, A* search shows how **smart estimation paired with actual cost can dramatically improve decision-making in complex environments**.

22. Minimax heuristic

The *Minimax heuristic* is a decision-making strategy used in game theory and artificial intelligence, especially in **two-player, turn-based, zero-sum games** like chess, tic-tac-toe, or checkers. The core idea is simple: assume that your opponent is playing optimally and try to **minimize the maximum possible loss** (hence "minimax"). This heuristic helps a player choose a move that leads to the best worst-case scenario, preparing for the most unfavourable response the opponent might make.

Originally formulated by **John von Neumann** in the 1940s and later formalized in AI by **Allen Newell and Herbert Simon**, the minimax heuristic is foundational in adversarial search algorithms. It doesn't guarantee the best outcome in every situation but ensures the safest move against a rational opponent.

Example

Consider a simple version of tic-tac-toe. If it's your move and you're considering placing your "X" in one of three empty spots, you simulate how your opponent would respond to each. For each of their potential responses, you predict your future counter-responses. You construct a tree of possible future states, alternating between your turn (trying to **maximize** your outcome) and your opponent's turn (trying to **minimize** your outcome). Using this structure, you choose the move that leads to the best possible outcome assuming your opponent is also playing smartly.

Why It Works

The minimax heuristic works because it incorporates the notion of **strategic foresight**. Rather than evaluating only immediate consequences, it anticipates counter-moves and considers how actions may play out over several turns. It's particularly useful in adversarial situations, where the outcome is not solely determined by your own decisions but also by your opponent's strategy.

It's a form of **robust decision-making**—assuming the worst from your opponent helps ensure your choices are defensible and less likely to result in a significant loss.

How It Works

1. **Tree Construction**: Build a decision tree representing all possible moves and countermoves.

2. **Terminal Evaluation**: Assign utility scores (e.g., win = +1, lose = −1, draw = 0) to end states.

3. **Backpropagation**: Starting from the terminal nodes, propagate values up the tree:

   o   Max nodes (your turn): choose the move with the highest score.

- o Min nodes (opponent's turn): assume they choose the move with the lowest score.

4. **Decision Point**: Select the move at the root that leads to the optimal minimax value.

Application

Minimax is widely used in **AI for board games** like chess, Go, and Othello. In combination with techniques like **alpha-beta pruning** (which reduces the number of nodes evaluated), it powers modern game-playing systems. It also has applications in **strategic planning**, **negotiation modelling**, and **cybersecurity**, where anticipating the moves of an adversary is essential.

Key Insights

- Minimax is best suited for competitive, zero-sum contexts.
- It prioritizes security and consistency over risk-taking.
- It becomes computationally expensive as game complexity increases.
- When paired with pruning and heuristics, it becomes highly efficient and powerful.

Ultimately, the minimax heuristic teaches us that in adversarial situations, **preparing for the smartest opponent leads to the smartest moves**.

23. Hill climbing heuristic

Hill climbing is a **local search heuristic** used in problem-solving and optimization. It is inspired by the idea of climbing a hill step-by-step, always choosing the next move that most increases value (or decreases cost), with the goal of reaching the highest peak (optimal solution). Unlike exhaustive search methods, hill climbing **does not look ahead** beyond the immediate neighbouring states, making it a **greedy, myopic algorithm**.

Hill climbing is commonly used in **artificial intelligence**, **operations research**, and **machine learning** for solving complex problems where the solution space is vast, and evaluating all possibilities is computationally infeasible.

Example

Imagine you're trying to reach the highest point on a mountain range while blindfolded. At each step, you feel your surroundings and move only to the neighbouring spot that feels higher than where you are now. You repeat this process until no adjacent step is higher. At that point, you assume you've reached the peak.

However, without seeing the entire landscape, you might stop at a smaller hill (local maximum) instead of the highest peak (global maximum). This analogy reflects the core limitation of hill climbing: it can **get stuck in local optima**.

Why It Works

Hill climbing works well because it is **simple, fast, and requires minimal memory**. It is especially effective when the solution space has a **smooth landscape** with a single peak or when local optima are rare or close to the global optimum.

The heuristic leverages **incremental improvement**—an efficient strategy when the evaluation function provides clear feedback on which direction is better. It is widely used because it doesn't require building a complete search tree or maintaining large lists of paths or states.

How It Works

1. **Start at an Initial State**: Choose a random or informed starting point.

2. **Evaluate Neighbours**: Assess adjacent or nearby states.

3. **Move to Best Neighbour**: If a neighbour has a higher value (or lower cost), move to that state.

4. **Repeat**: Continue this process until no neighbour is better.

5. **Stop Condition**: If all adjacent states are worse or equal, the search terminates—this is the current peak.

Variants like **stochastic hill climbing**, **random-restart hill climbing**, and **simulated annealing** attempt to overcome the risk of getting stuck in local optima.

Application

Hill climbing is used in **robot path planning**, **schedule optimization**, **machine learning hyperparameter tuning**, and even **video game AI**. For example, in logistics, it can help optimize delivery routes based on minimizing distance or fuel consumption.

In **AI game agents**, hill climbing allows characters to pursue better strategies incrementally without simulating every possibility.

Key Insights

- Hill climbing is efficient and easy to implement but **can fail to find global optima**.

- It's best used when the problem landscape is relatively smooth or well-understood.

- Enhancements like **random restarts** or combining it with **probabilistic jumps** improve robustness.

- It teaches a powerful lesson: **incremental improvement is effective—but sometimes you need to step back to move forward.**

24. Beam search heuristic

Beam Search Heuristic

Beam search is a heuristic search algorithm used to explore large solution spaces efficiently by **limiting the number of paths** considered at each step. It is a **breadth-limited version of best-first search**, where only the k most promising candidates—known as the *beam width*—are kept for further expansion. This makes beam search a powerful compromise between exhaustive search and greedy methods, particularly useful when dealing with **combinatorially large problems**.

Beam search is commonly used in **natural language processing (NLP)**, **speech recognition**, **machine translation**, and **robotics**, where generating or selecting the best possible sequence or decision path is computationally intensive.

Example

Consider a text prediction task, where the system must generate the most likely sentence continuation: "The cat sat on the..." The model might consider many words ("mat," "floor," "roof," "dog," etc.). Instead of expanding *all* possible continuations, beam search keeps only the top k candidates with the highest probability after each word addition.

If the beam width is 3, it will retain only the three most likely partial sentences at each stage, pruning the rest. This prevents exponential growth in possibilities and narrows the focus to the most promising paths, improving speed and efficiency without entirely sacrificing quality.

Why It Works

Beam search works well because it **prioritizes promising solutions** while maintaining diversity through multiple candidates. Unlike greedy algorithms that pursue the single best path (risking dead ends), beam search retains several alternatives, reducing the likelihood of missing good solutions due to early mistakes.

The balance between **exploration and exploitation** makes it particularly effective in domains where early choices strongly influence final outcomes—like sentence generation or planning in dynamic environments.

How It Works

1. **Initialize**: Start from a root or initial state.

2. **Expand**: Generate all possible successors for each state in the current beam.

3. **Score**: Evaluate each successor using a heuristic or probability function.

4. **Prune**: Keep only the top k candidates based on their scores (beam width).

5. **Repeat**: Continue expanding and pruning until the goal state is reached or a stopping criterion is met.

The beam width k controls the trade-off between **efficiency** and **accuracy**—larger beams explore more, but are slower.

Application

In **machine translation**, beam search selects the most probable sequence of words to translate a sentence from one language to another. In **robot navigation**, it helps identify optimal movement sequences by evaluating only a manageable number of paths. It's also used in **speech recognition** and **autocomplete systems**, where it predicts the next words based on current input.

Key Insights

- Beam search balances breadth and depth by restricting exploration to top candidates.

- It's faster and more scalable than exhaustive search, but not guaranteed to find the optimal solution.

- The choice of beam width critically affects performance: too narrow may miss good paths; too wide becomes inefficient.

- It excels in sequential decision-making tasks where early errors compound over time.

Ultimately, beam search shows that **smart pruning can lead to smart solutions—especially when perfection is impractical.**

25. Simulated annealing heuristic

Simulated annealing is a probabilistic optimization heuristic inspired by **metallurgy**, specifically the process of heating and slowly cooling metal to remove defects and optimize its internal structure. Introduced in the 1980s by **Kirkpatrick, Gelatt, and Vecchi**, the algorithm mimics this process to find near-optimal solutions in complex, high-dimensional search spaces.

It is particularly useful in problems with **many local optima**, where simpler methods like hill climbing may get stuck. Simulated annealing overcomes this by occasionally allowing *worse* moves, helping it escape local optima and explore the solution space more broadly before gradually "cooling down" into a final, refined answer.

Example

Imagine you're trying to minimize the travel distance in the **Traveling Salesman Problem (TSP)**—where a salesman must visit a list of cities and return to the starting point while minimizing total distance. A greedy or hill climbing approach might settle on a short route early but miss a much better one hidden deeper in the search space.

Simulated annealing starts with an initial tour and iteratively makes small changes (e.g., swapping two cities). If the new tour is shorter, it's accepted. If it's longer, it might *still* be accepted with a certain probability. Over time, this probability decreases, reducing the likelihood of accepting worse solutions and leading the algorithm to settle near an optimal route.

Why It Works

Simulated annealing works because it balances **exploration** (searching broadly across the solution space) with **exploitation** (refining good solutions). By allowing occasional uphill moves— where the solution gets worse—it avoids premature convergence on local optima. As the "temperature" lowers, the algorithm becomes more conservative, settling into areas of high-quality solutions.

The metaphor of temperature and cooling captures this dynamic shift from global exploration to local optimization.

How It Works

1. **Initialization**: Start with an initial solution and a high temperature.

2. **Perturbation**: Make a small random change to the current solution.

3. **Evaluation**: Calculate the difference in cost (ΔE) between new and current solution.

4. **Acceptance Rule**:

   o   If $\Delta E < 0$ (better), accept the new solution.

   o   If $\Delta E > 0$ (worse), accept with probability $e^{\wedge}(-\Delta E/T)$.

5. **Cooling Schedule**: Gradually decrease temperature T according to a predefined schedule.

6. **Repeat**: Continue until temperature is near zero or a stopping condition is met.

Application

Simulated annealing is widely used in **combinatorial optimization** problems like **scheduling, network design, VLSI layout, portfolio optimization**, and **machine learning hyperparameter tuning**. It's especially helpful when the problem space is rugged or poorly understood.

Key Insights

- Simulated annealing avoids local optima by accepting worse solutions early on.

- Its success heavily depends on the **cooling schedule** and **perturbation strategy**.

- It doesn't guarantee a global optimum but often gets *very close*.

- It's versatile and can be applied to almost any optimization problem with a definable cost function.

In essence, simulated annealing teaches us that **a little randomness early on can lead to better decisions later**.

26. Genetic algorithm fitness heuristic

The *Genetic Algorithm (GA) fitness heuristic* is a key component of genetic algorithms—adaptive, search-based optimization techniques inspired by the principles of **natural selection** and **evolutionary biology**. Developed by **John Holland** in the 1970s, genetic algorithms simulate the process of evolution to find optimal or near-optimal solutions to complex problems. The **fitness heuristic** is central to how solutions are evaluated and selected for "survival" and reproduction in this process.

Fitness refers to how well a candidate solution (or *individual*) solves the problem at hand. The heuristic provides a **quantitative score** that guides the algorithm's selection process. Better-performing individuals are more likely to be retained and combined to produce the next generation, gradually improving the population over time.

Example

Suppose you're trying to design the most aerodynamic shape for a drone. Each potential shape is encoded as a string of parameters (a *chromosome*). The fitness heuristic could be based on how far the drone flies using that shape, or how much energy it consumes.

Each generation, you evaluate every candidate's performance using this fitness score. Shapes that perform better are more likely to be "mated" (crossover) or "mutated" to produce new designs. Over many generations, you evolve toward a highly optimized drone shape.

Why It Works

The fitness heuristic works because it **quantifies quality** in a domain-appropriate way, allowing the algorithm to favour better solutions without needing a detailed, rule-based understanding of the problem. By selectively amplifying successful traits (high fitness) and discarding poor ones (low fitness), the system mimics biological evolution to gradually explore and exploit the solution space.

This process supports **exploration (diversity)** and **exploitation (refinement)**—key ingredients in efficient problem-solving under uncertainty or complexity.

How It Works

1. **Initialization**: Generate an initial population of random candidate solutions.

2. **Fitness Evaluation**: Use a heuristic function to assign a fitness score to each individual.

3. **Selection**: Choose individuals based on their fitness— higher scores mean higher selection probability.

4. **Crossover**: Combine parts of two "parent" solutions to create "offspring."

5. **Mutation**: Introduce small random changes to maintain diversity.

6. **Replacement**: Form a new generation using selected offspring.

7. **Repeat**: Continue the process until a stopping condition is met (e.g., max generations or satisfactory fitness).

Application

Genetic algorithms with fitness heuristics are used in **engineering design, machine learning, robotics, automated scheduling, financial modelling**, and **game development**. For example, they optimize neural network architectures, discover efficient supply chain routes, or tune trading strategies based on market performance.

Key Insights

- The fitness function drives the entire evolutionary process—its design is crucial.

- GAs balance randomness with guided improvement, making them resilient to local optima.

- Fitness-based selection ensures that progress is both adaptive and directional.

- They are especially useful in domains where traditional optimization fails due to complexity or non-linearity.

In essence, the genetic algorithm fitness heuristic shows that **evolution isn't just biological—it's computational, too**.

27. Greedy algorithm heuristic

The *greedy algorithm* heuristic is a problem-solving strategy that builds up a solution piece by piece, always choosing the **locally optimal choice** at each step with the hope that this leads to a **globally optimal solution**. Greedy algorithms are simple, intuitive, and efficient, making them a popular tool in both theoretical computer science and practical applications.

The core assumption behind this heuristic is that **locally optimal decisions lead to globally optimal outcomes**—though this isn't always guaranteed. It works best in problems that exhibit the **greedy-choice property** (where local choices lead to global optima) and **optimal substructure** (where optimal solutions contain optimal sub-solutions).

Example

A classic example is the **coin change problem**: Suppose you need to make 63 cents using the fewest coins, and you have denominations of 1, 5, 10, 25, and 50 cents. A greedy algorithm would choose the largest denomination that doesn't exceed the amount at each step: one 50¢ coin, one 10¢ coin, and three 1¢ coins.

This works for standard U.S. coin systems. However, in some coin systems, the greedy choice can fail to give the fewest coins— demonstrating that greedy algorithms don't always produce the optimal solution unless the problem structure supports it.

Why It Works

Greedy algorithms work well when:

- The problem has **optimal substructure** (a global solution can be built from local solutions).

- The **greedy-choice property** holds (making local optimal choices leads to a globally optimal solution).

- Speed is more important than absolute accuracy.

They are especially useful because they **minimize computation**, often operating in linear or logarithmic time, compared to exhaustive methods like dynamic programming.

How It Works

1. **Initialization**: Start with an empty solution.

2. **Greedy Selection**: Choose the best available option at the moment (based on a heuristic such as lowest cost, highest value, shortest path, etc.).

3. **Feasibility Check**: Ensure the choice doesn't violate problem constraints.

4. **Iteration**: Add the choice to the solution and move to the next step.

5. **Termination**: Repeat until the full solution is constructed or no choices remain.

Application

Greedy algorithms are used in:

- **Graph algorithms**: Dijkstra's shortest path, Prim's minimum spanning tree.

- **Scheduling problems**: Assigning jobs to machines based on earliest deadlines or shortest processing time.

- **Compression**: Huffman coding for optimal data encoding.

- **Resource allocation**: Greedy strategies for maximizing profit or minimizing cost under constraints.

Key Insights

- Greedy algorithms are fast and memory-efficient, ideal for real-time or large-scale problems.

- They don't always produce the optimal solution—but when they do, they do so with impressive simplicity.

- Understanding the problem's structure is key to knowing whether the greedy approach will succeed.

- Greedy methods teach that **sometimes, "best at the moment" can be enough**—especially when time is limited.

In summary, the greedy algorithm heuristic reminds us that **thinking small, step by step, can sometimes solve big problems—efficiently**.

28. Heuristic pruning heuristic

Heuristic pruning is a decision-making strategy used in search algorithms to **narrow down the number of paths or options explored** by eliminating those that appear unlikely to lead to a desirable or optimal outcome. This approach uses heuristics— experience-based rules or educated guesses—to "prune" or cut off large parts of the decision tree, thereby reducing computational effort.

Heuristic pruning is particularly useful in **complex or high-dimensional search spaces**, where evaluating every possible path is computationally impractical. It is widely applied in areas such as **game theory, artificial intelligence (AI), robotics, and constraint satisfaction problems**.

Example

In **chess AI**, heuristic pruning helps reduce the vast number of potential moves a computer must evaluate. For instance, in a given position, the AI might evaluate only those moves that result in material gain, avoid immediate threats, or control the centre—while ignoring others that heuristically seem less promising. By pruning unlikely moves early, the AI can look deeper into the more promising lines without being overwhelmed by irrelevant options.

A famous example is **alpha-beta pruning**, which is often used in conjunction with the minimax algorithm to eliminate branches in the game tree that don't need to be explored because they can't affect the final decision.

Why It Works

Heuristic pruning works because not all paths are equally promising, and real-world problems often exhibit **patterns or regularities** that can be exploited. By incorporating domain-specific knowledge or statistical patterns, pruning helps focus computational resources where they matter most. This approach dramatically **reduces complexity** without significantly compromising the quality of the solution.

It also reflects how humans make decisions—we don't consider every possible action but rather eliminate many options intuitively based on experience or rules of thumb.

How It Works

1. **Search Initialization**: Begin exploring a decision or search tree.

2. **Heuristic Evaluation**: At each node, use a heuristic to score or assess future branches.

3. **Pruning Decision**: If a branch is unlikely to yield a better result than already-explored options, discard it.

4. **Focused Exploration**: Continue expanding only the most promising branches.

5. **Solution Selection**: Choose the best outcome from the reduced search space.

This approach allows deeper exploration of useful paths without being bogged down by irrelevant ones.

Application

In **AI planning** and **robot navigation**, heuristic pruning reduces pathfinding time in complex environments. In **automated theorem proving**, it eliminates logically unproductive paths. In **natural language processing**, it helps limit combinatorial explosion when parsing sentences or generating language.

Key Insights

*   Heuristic pruning dramatically improves efficiency in large or complex decision spaces.

*   It's most effective when paired with reliable domain-specific heuristics.

*   It may not guarantee the optimal solution but offers **fast, near-optimal performance**.

*   Like human intuition, it favors **selective depth over exhaustive breadth**.

In essence, heuristic pruning reminds us that **strategically ignoring can be just as powerful as knowing what to explore**.

29. Tabu search heuristic

Tabu Search is a **metaheuristic optimization algorithm** that guides local search methods to escape local optima by maintaining a short-term memory of recently visited solutions—called the *tabu list*. Developed by **Fred Glover in the 1980s**, this strategy allows the search to continue even when no immediate improvement is available, by permitting non-improving moves under controlled conditions.

Unlike greedy algorithms or basic hill climbing, which stop at the first local optimum, Tabu Search allows exploration beyond local peaks. It's particularly powerful for solving **combinatorial optimization problems**, where the solution space is large and full of traps like plateaus and local maxima.

Example

Imagine trying to find the shortest route for a traveling salesman who must visit multiple cities (the Traveling Salesman Problem). Starting with an initial tour, the algorithm evaluates nearby solutions (e.g., swapping two cities in the sequence). If a new solution improves the total distance, it's accepted. If not, the algorithm might still accept it to escape stagnation.

To prevent cycling back to previously visited poor solutions, recent moves (like specific city swaps) are placed on a *tabu list*— a temporary memory that prohibits reversing those moves for a fixed number of iterations, unless doing so meets an overriding aspiration criterion (e.g., leading to a new best solution).

Why It Works

Tabu Search works because it introduces **strategic exploration** into local search. By allowing non-improving moves and preventing reversal of recent decisions, it avoids getting trapped in suboptimal areas of the search space. It also balances **diversification** (exploring new regions) and **intensification** (refining good areas) through its memory structures.

Its flexible memory system allows it to adapt its behaviour over time, adjusting how it searches and which moves it prioritizes, making it robust across many problem types.

How It Works

1. **Initialization**: Begin with a feasible solution and empty tabu list.

2. **Neighbourhood Evaluation**: Generate a set of candidate moves (neighbouring solutions).

3. **Move Selection**: Choose the best move that is *not* on the tabu list—or override tabu status if an aspiration condition is met.

4. **Update**: Apply the move, update the current solution, and refresh the tabu list.

5. **Termination**: Repeat until a stopping condition is met (e.g., time limit, max iterations, or satisfactory solution).

The tabu list typically stores recently made changes, not whole solutions, making it memory-efficient.

Application

Tabu Search is widely used in **scheduling, routing, timetabling, resource allocation**, and **network design**. For example, airlines use it to schedule crews, logistics companies use it for delivery routing, and manufacturers apply it for machine job assignments.

Key Insights

- Tabu Search enables escape from local optima through flexible memory and adaptive rules.

- It's effective for complex, real-world problems where traditional methods fail.

- Performance depends on designing effective neighbourhood structures and aspiration criteria.

- It shows that sometimes, **accepting a setback is the best way forward** in search.

In essence, Tabu Search reveals the power of *strategic forgetting and controlled exploration* in solving hard optimization problems.

30. Heuristic function in constraint satisfaction heuristic

In **Constraint Satisfaction Problems (CSPs)**—such as scheduling, resource allocation, and puzzle solving—a *heuristic function* is used to guide the search process toward more promising solutions by intelligently selecting variables and values during problem-solving. Rather than exploring the entire search space exhaustively, heuristic functions reduce computational effort by prioritizing decisions likely to lead to solutions.

A CSP typically involves:

- A set of **variables**

- A **domain** of possible values for each variable

- A set of **constraints** that specify allowable combinations of values

The heuristic function serves as a strategy to navigate this space effectively, using informed rules or patterns to prune less promising paths and focus on likely candidates.

Example

Consider the **map colouring problem**, where adjacent regions must be coloured differently using a limited number of colours. A basic approach might test every colour combination, but this is computationally expensive. A heuristic function could apply strategies like:

- **Minimum Remaining Values (MRV)**: Choose the variable with the fewest legal values left.

- **Degree Heuristic**: Choose the variable involved in the largest number of constraints with unassigned variables.

- **Least Constraining Value (LCV)**: Choose the value that rules out the fewest options for neighbouring variables.

By applying these heuristics, a solver might assign colours to difficult regions early, reducing failure and backtracking later.

Why It Works

Heuristic functions work in CSPs because they **exploit structure** in the problem. Some variables are more critical to resolve early, and some values are less likely to create conflicts. By making smarter decisions at each step, heuristics reduce the search space and increase the likelihood of finding a consistent assignment quickly.

This guided search avoids the inefficiency of brute-force approaches while maintaining completeness and soundness when integrated with backtracking algorithms.

How It Works

1. **Variable Selection**: Use heuristics like MRV or degree to pick the next variable to assign.

2. **Value Selection**: Use heuristics like LCV to decide which value to try first.

3. **Constraint Propagation**: Apply algorithms like forward checking or arc consistency to eliminate conflicting values from other variables.

4. **Search and Backtrack**: Continue exploring, backtracking when constraints are violated.

The heuristic function dynamically adapts the search based on partial assignments and constraint relationships.

Application

Heuristic functions are central in solving CSPs such as:

- **Sudoku** and other logic puzzles

- **Exam and course timetabling**

- **AI planning and robotics**

- **Resource allocation in manufacturing or cloud computing**

They are also used in AI algorithms for **natural language understanding**, **configuration problems**, and **diagnostic systems**.

Key Insights

- Heuristics guide CSP solvers to faster, more efficient solutions by prioritizing high-impact decisions.

- They significantly reduce backtracking and time complexity in large-scale problems.

- Combining multiple heuristics often leads to more robust performance.

- They demonstrate how **problem-specific knowledge can dramatically improve general search strategies**.

In short, heuristic functions in CSPs show how **smart choices, not exhaustive ones, solve complex problems efficiently**.

31. Divide and conquer heuristic

Divide and conquer is a powerful problem-solving heuristic and algorithm design paradigm that involves breaking a complex problem into smaller, more manageable sub-problems, solving each independently, and then combining their solutions to address the original problem. It reflects the cognitive strategy of handling complexity by **partitioning** rather than tackling the whole problem at once.

This approach is foundational in both **computer science** and **cognitive psychology**, where it's used to improve efficiency, clarity, and tractability in problem-solving.

Example

One of the most famous examples is **Merge Sort**, a sorting algorithm that uses divide and conquer. Given a list of numbers to sort, the algorithm:

1. **Divides** the list into two halves,

2. **Recursively sorts** each half, and

3. **Merges** the two sorted halves back together.

This method reduces the complexity from the brute-force $O(n^2)$ to $O(n \log n)$, illustrating how divide and conquer can drastically enhance efficiency.

Why It Works

Divide and conquer works because it **reduces problem size**, which simplifies computation. Smaller sub-problems are easier and faster to solve, and they often exhibit patterns or structure that can be exploited more easily than in the larger problem. Moreover, many complex problems are *recursive in nature*—they can be defined in terms of smaller instances of themselves.

It also enhances parallelism: sub-problems can often be solved independently, making this approach well-suited for **multi-core or distributed computing** environments.

From a psychological perspective, it reflects how humans naturally manage complexity—by breaking tasks into chunks or stages.

How It Works

1. **Divide**: Partition the problem into smaller, similar sub-problems.

2. **Conquer**: Solve each sub-problem recursively. If a sub-problem is small enough, solve it directly.

3. **Combine**: Merge or integrate the solutions to the sub-problems to form the final result.

The effectiveness of this method often depends on how well the division step simplifies the original problem and whether the combining step is efficient.

Application

Divide and conquer is ubiquitous:

- In **computer science**, it underpins algorithms like Quick Sort, Merge Sort, Binary Search, and Fast Fourier Transform.

- In **mathematics**, it's used to solve recurrence relations and factor large numbers.

- In **problem-solving and planning**, people use it to tackle complex projects (e.g., breaking a report into sections or a product launch into phases).

- In **AI**, it assists in search algorithms, decision trees, and game-playing strategies.

Key Insights

- Divide and conquer leverages structure and recursion to simplify complex tasks.

- It promotes clarity, reusability, and parallelism.

- The approach is efficient when sub-problems are independent and the combine step is straightforward.

- It teaches a general lesson: **solving parts well often leads to solving the whole effectively**.

In essence, divide and conquer demonstrates that **breaking down is often the key to building up**—in both computing and cognition.

32. Backtracking heuristic

The *backtracking heuristic* is a problem-solving strategy used to **systematically explore** all possible configurations of a solution by trying partial solutions and abandoning them as soon as it's clear they won't lead to a viable outcome. It is a **depth-first search** technique that incorporates trial and error along with the ability to "backtrack"—to reverse decisions and try new paths.

This heuristic is particularly useful in **constraint satisfaction problems (CSPs)**, such as puzzles, scheduling, or pathfinding, where the solution must satisfy a set of conditions. It is not purely blind trial and error; when enhanced with intelligent heuristics, it becomes highly efficient.

Example

A classic example is solving a **Sudoku puzzle**. The algorithm begins by placing a number in the first empty cell and recursively attempts to fill in the rest. If a conflict arises (e.g., a duplicate number in a row), it backtracks—removing the last placed number—and tries the next valid option. This continues until the board is correctly filled or all options are exhausted.

Why It Works

Backtracking works because it avoids pursuing invalid paths to their conclusion. Rather than brute-force evaluating every complete solution, it identifies and **eliminates failing partial**

solutions early, greatly reducing the search space. This is especially effective when combined with **heuristics** that prioritize the most promising paths first (e.g., choosing variables with the fewest legal values left).

It mimics how humans solve complex logical problems: we try, assess, and revise when necessary. Its strength lies in flexibility and its ability to recover from poor decisions without restarting the entire process.

How It Works

1. **Start with an empty solution**: Begin by selecting a starting point.

2. **Make a choice**: Assign a value to a variable or take a step forward.

3. **Check constraints**: If the current partial solution violates constraints, **backtrack**.

4. **Recursive exploration**: Proceed recursively with the next variable or decision.

5. **Backtrack as needed**: If no valid options are left, undo the last step and try an alternative.

6. **Repeat** until a full valid solution is found or all paths are exhausted.

Heuristics like **forward checking, minimum remaining values (MRV)**, and **degree heuristics** can guide this process, making it far more efficient than naive exploration.

Application

Backtracking is widely used in:

- **Puzzle solving** (e.g., Sudoku, n-queens, crosswords)

- **CSPs** (e.g., scheduling exams, assigning resources)

- **Game AI** (e.g., exploring move sequences in board games)

- **Pathfinding and navigation** in constrained environments

- **Combinatorial generation**, such as permutations or valid string formations

Key Insights

- Backtracking is systematic and complete—it will find a solution if one exists.

- It avoids unnecessary computation by cutting off invalid paths early.

- The effectiveness increases significantly with well-chosen variable/value heuristics.

- It exemplifies the principle that **strategic reversal can be more efficient than exhaustive effort**.

Ultimately, backtracking demonstrates that **intelligent trial and error—guided by structure and rules—can solve even the most complex puzzles**.

33. Iterative deepening heuristic

Iterative Deepening (also known as **Iterative Deepening Depth-First Search**, or IDDFS) is a hybrid heuristic search strategy that combines the **space efficiency of depth-first search (DFS)** with the **completeness and optimality of breadth-first search (BFS)**. It works by repeatedly running a depth-limited search with increasing depth limits, progressively expanding the search horizon until a goal is found.

This approach is particularly useful in domains where the solution depth is unknown and memory constraints are significant. It is often applied in artificial intelligence, especially in **game-playing agents**, **robotics**, and **pathfinding**.

Example

Imagine a robot trying to find the shortest path through a maze to reach a goal. It doesn't know how far the goal is, and using BFS would consume too much memory to store every node at each level. Iterative deepening starts by searching to depth 1. If no solution is found, it searches to depth 2, then depth 3, and so on. Each iteration re-explores the search tree from the root but only up to the new depth limit. Eventually, the goal is reached at the shallowest possible depth, ensuring optimality.

Why It Works

Iterative deepening works because in many tree-like structures, **most nodes are located near the leaves**, not near the root. Although the early nodes are revisited multiple times, the number of nodes at shallow depths is relatively small compared to deeper levels. As a result, the repeated work is minimal compared to the savings in memory and the benefit of finding the shallowest solution.

It effectively sidesteps the **memory limitations** of BFS and the **incompleteness and potential infinite loops** of DFS.

How It Works

1. **Set Depth Limit**: Start with a depth limit of 0.

2. **Depth-Limited Search (DLS)**: Perform DFS up to the current depth limit.

3. **Check for Goal**: If the goal is found, return the path.

4. **Increment Depth**: If not, increase the limit by 1 and repeat DLS.

5. **Repeat** until the goal is found or the space is exhausted.

IDDFS guarantees to find the optimal solution (in terms of depth) if one exists.

Application

Iterative deepening is used in:

- **Game-tree searches** (e.g., chess engines like Deep Blue)

- **AI planning systems**

- **Pathfinding in unknown environments**

- **Problem-solving agents** in deterministic, single-agent scenarios

In **real-time AI**, it is often used in conjunction with **iterative deepening A*** (IDA*) for weighted graph searches.

Key Insights

- IDDFS is both **complete** and **optimal** (like BFS), but **space-efficient** (like DFS).

- It avoids the pitfalls of DFS (getting stuck in deep or infinite branches) and the heavy memory demands of BFS.

- The overhead of repeated exploration is offset by scalability and robustness.

- It reflects the idea that **solving complex problems incrementally can be more efficient than diving deep from the start**.

Ultimately, iterative deepening shows that **patience and repetition, applied systematically, can outperform brute force in constrained environments**.

34. Gradient descent (with heuristic tuning)

Gradient descent is an optimization algorithm widely used in machine learning and mathematical modelling to find the **minimum of a function**. The idea is to iteratively adjust parameters in the direction that most rapidly decreases the error or loss—based on the gradient (slope) of the function.

When enhanced with **heuristic tuning**, gradient descent incorporates rule-of-thumb strategies to improve convergence speed, avoid local minima, and balance learning rate. These heuristics—such as momentum, adaptive learning rates, or scheduled decay—are not derived from first principles but from practical experience in optimizing complex models.

Example

Consider training a neural network to classify images. Gradient descent adjusts the weights and biases of the network by calculating how much a small change in each parameter would reduce the error on the training set. However, if the learning rate is too high, the algorithm might overshoot the optimal values; if too low, it will take too long or get stuck.

Here's where **heuristic tuning** comes in: using strategies like **learning rate schedules**, **momentum**, or **Adam optimizer**—which adapts the learning rate based on past gradients—to improve performance without requiring extensive manual tuning.

Why It Works

Gradient descent works because it follows the principle of **local optimization**—moving in the direction of steepest descent based on current knowledge. Heuristic tuning improves this by **dynamically adapting** the way the descent behaves, helping it to:

- Avoid overshooting the minimum
- Escape flat regions or local minima
- Converge more quickly

Heuristics such as adaptive learning rates work well because real-world optimization landscapes are often irregular, with steep slopes, plateaus, and multiple minima.

How It Works

1. **Initialize**: Start with random values for parameters (e.g., weights in a model).
2. **Compute Gradient**: Use the derivative of the loss function to determine the direction of steepest ascent.
3. **Update Parameters**: Adjust parameters in the opposite direction of the gradient using a learning rate.

- o With heuristic tuning, modify the learning rate or add terms like momentum.

4. **Repeat**: Iterate this process until the model converges or improvement stalls.

Heuristic tuning may involve:

- **Momentum**: Adds a fraction of the previous update to smooth changes.

- **Learning Rate Schedules**: Reduce learning rate over time to fine-tune convergence.

- **Adaptive Methods**: (e.g., RMSprop, Adam) that adjust learning rates per parameter.

Application

Gradient descent with heuristic tuning is essential in:

- **Training neural networks** and deep learning models

- **Regression analysis**

- **Convex optimization**

- **Natural language processing and computer vision**

These techniques are built into machine learning libraries like TensorFlow, PyTorch, and scikit-learn.

Key Insights

- Gradient descent is powerful, but naïve implementations can be inefficient or unstable.

- Heuristic tuning transforms gradient descent into a **robust, scalable optimizer**.

- Adaptive strategies reduce the burden of manual tuning and make models more generalizable.

- It reflects a balance between **mathematical rigor and empirical strategy**.

Ultimately, gradient descent with heuristic tuning shows that **smart shortcuts can make sophisticated learning both faster and more reliable**.

35. Nearest neighbour heuristic

The *Nearest Neighbour* heuristic is a simple, greedy algorithm used primarily for **combinatorial optimization** problems, such as route planning and spatial search. The central idea is straightforward: starting from an initial point, always move to the **closest unvisited neighbour**, repeating this process until all points have been visited.

This heuristic is particularly well-known for its application to the **Traveling Salesman Problem (TSP)**, where the objective is to find the shortest possible route that visits each city once and returns to the starting point.

Example

Suppose a delivery driver must drop off packages at 10 locations. Starting at the depot, the driver uses the nearest neighbour heuristic by selecting the closest delivery point, travels there, and then proceeds to the next closest unvisited point. This continues until all packages are delivered and the driver returns to the depot.

Although this method does not guarantee the shortest overall route, it produces a **quick and reasonable** path with minimal computational effort—especially important in time-constrained situations.

Why It Works

The nearest neighbour heuristic works because it prioritizes **local efficiency**, reducing the immediate cost at each step. In many real-world problems, especially when the number of elements is large, calculating the globally optimal solution is **computationally expensive** or infeasible. The nearest neighbour approach trades off some level of accuracy for speed and simplicity.

It is particularly useful in domains where:

- Solutions are needed quickly.

- Slight inefficiencies are acceptable.

- Computational resources are limited.

How It Works

1. **Start at an initial point** (e.g., origin city or depot).

2. **Find the nearest unvisited neighbour** using a distance metric (e.g., Euclidean distance).

3. **Move to that neighbour** and mark it as visited.

4. **Repeat** steps 2–3 until all points have been visited.

5. **Optionally return to the starting point** to complete a loop (as in TSP).

This greedy approach builds the path incrementally, always making the "best" move available at the time.

Application

The nearest neighbour heuristic is used in:

- **Routing and logistics** (e.g., delivery planning, ride-sharing, and mail distribution).

- **Geographic information systems (GIS)** for clustering and proximity analysis.

- **Pattern recognition** and **machine learning**, especially in the *k-nearest neighbours* (KNN) algorithm, where classification is based on proximity in feature space.

- **Network design**, such as laying out shortest cabling paths or constructing low-cost sensor networks.

Key Insights

- The nearest neighbour heuristic is fast and easy to implement, making it ideal for real-time decision-making.

- It **does not guarantee an optimal solution** and can sometimes yield poor performance in specific layouts.

- It's often used as a **baseline** or as a component in more complex algorithms (e.g., genetic algorithms, simulated annealing).

- Enhancements like **restarting from different points** or **2-opt optimization** can significantly improve results.

In essence, the nearest neighbour heuristic shows that **greedy local decisions can yield useful global approximations**, especially when speed and simplicity matter most.

36. Metaheuristics heuristic

Metaheuristics are high-level strategies designed to guide and control lower-level heuristics to effectively explore large and complex search spaces. They are used for solving **optimization problems** where exact methods are too computationally expensive or impractical. Unlike simple heuristics that exploit local information, metaheuristics incorporate mechanisms for **exploration, diversification, and escape from local optima.**

The term *metaheuristic* means "beyond heuristics," emphasizing its role as a general problem-solving framework rather than a specific, rigid algorithm. Metaheuristics are **problem-independent**, adaptable across domains, and often inspired by natural or biological processes.

Example

A classic example is the **Genetic Algorithm (GA)**, a metaheuristic inspired by natural evolution. It works by maintaining a population of candidate solutions, selecting the fittest individuals, and applying genetic operators (crossover and mutation) to evolve better solutions over time.

Another example is **Simulated Annealing**, which mimics the cooling process in metallurgy, accepting both improving and (occasionally) worsening moves to escape local minima.

Why It Works

Metaheuristics work because they are designed to balance two competing goals in search:

1. **Exploration**: Searching new, unvisited regions of the solution space.

2. **Exploitation**: Refining known good regions to find optimal or near-optimal solutions.

Unlike simple local search or greedy algorithms, metaheuristics use strategies like randomization, adaptive memory, and probabilistic decision rules to **avoid getting stuck in suboptimal areas**. They do not require derivatives or problem-specific models, making them ideal for complex, noisy, or non-linear problems.

How It Works

Metaheuristics typically follow this generalized process:

1. **Initialization**: Generate one or more starting solutions (often randomly).

2. **Evaluation**: Use an objective function or heuristic to assess solution quality.

3. **Modification**: Apply operators (e.g., mutation, recombination, neighbourhood moves).

4. **Selection**: Choose the best or most promising solutions for the next iteration.

5. **Termination**: Stop after a predefined number of iterations, convergence, or time limit.

Different metaheuristics (e.g., Ant Colony Optimization, Particle Swarm Optimization, Tabu Search) implement these steps in domain-specific ways but share the same foundational logic.

Application

Metaheuristics are widely used in:

-   **Engineering design** (e.g., aerodynamic modelling, circuit design)

-   **Operations research** (e.g., vehicle routing, facility layout)

-   **Machine learning** (e.g., hyperparameter tuning, feature selection)

-   **Finance** (e.g., portfolio optimization, risk management)

They are especially useful when exact algorithms are too slow or the search space is poorly understood.

Key Insights

-   Metaheuristics are **flexible and powerful** for solving hard, real-world optimization problems.

-   They prioritize **good-enough solutions fast**, not perfection.

- Their strength lies in adaptability, making them applicable across industries.

- They teach that **structured randomness and guided experimentation** can outperform rigid logic when facing complexity.

In essence, metaheuristics show that **knowing how to search is sometimes more important than knowing exactly where to look**.

37. Subgoal decomposition heuristic

Subgoal decomposition is a cognitive and computational heuristic used to simplify complex problem-solving by **breaking down a primary goal into smaller, more manageable subgoals**. Rather than attempting to achieve a large objective all at once, this strategy focuses on solving one component at a time, progressively working toward the overall solution. It is rooted in human problem-solving theory and formalized in cognitive psychology through frameworks like **Means-End Analysis** and **Hierarchical Task Analysis**.

This approach is especially effective in environments where the goal is not immediately achievable and requires a sequence of intermediate steps—often found in planning, programming, robotics, and everyday decision-making.

Example

Consider the problem of organizing a conference. The main goal—hosting a successful event—can be overwhelming. By using subgoal decomposition, the task is broken into smaller parts: booking a venue, inviting speakers, setting up registration, arranging catering, etc. Each subgoal can then be tackled individually, often by different people or teams, eventually leading to the accomplishment of the larger goal.

In artificial intelligence, particularly in **automated planning**, this concept appears in **goal-based agents** that decompose a complex task (like assembling a product) into sequential actions and constraints.

Why It Works

Subgoal decomposition works because it **reduces cognitive load** and enables **focused attention** on smaller, solvable parts of a larger challenge. By turning a vague or complex goal into a series of concrete objectives, it increases clarity, structure, and motivation. It also allows for incremental progress—important in dynamic or resource-constrained settings where real-time adjustments are needed.

From a computational perspective, it narrows the search space by structuring it hierarchically, making problem-solving more efficient.

How It Works

1. **Define the Main Goal**: Clearly identify the overall objective.

2. **Identify Subgoals**: Break the goal into a logical sequence of smaller tasks or checkpoints.

3. **Plan for Each Subgoal**: Create actionable steps or assign tasks to achieve each subgoal.

4. **Solve Subgoals Sequentially or in Parallel**: Depending on dependencies, address subgoals in order or simultaneously.

5. **Integrate Solutions**: Combine completed subgoals to achieve the overall objective.

This approach can be implemented manually (e.g., to-do lists) or algorithmically in AI systems (e.g., STRIPS planning).

Application

Subgoal decomposition is fundamental in:

- **Software engineering** (breaking large programs into modules)

- **Robotics and AI** (task planning and behaviour trees)

- **Education** (breaking learning objectives into smaller concepts)

- **Project management** (Gantt charts and work breakdown structures)

In **cognitive psychology**, it's used to explain human reasoning in problem-solving tasks like puzzle-solving or mathematical proofs.

Key Insights

- Breaking a large goal into subgoals simplifies planning and execution.

- It enhances **problem clarity, progress monitoring**, and **resource allocation**.

- It supports both **human cognition** and **algorithmic efficiency**.

- Subgoal decomposition teaches that **progress is best made one clear step at a time**, especially when the whole picture feels overwhelming.

In essence, it demonstrates that **clarity through structure is the foundation of effective problem-solving**.

38. Rule-of-thumb estimates heuristic

The *rule-of-thumb estimates* heuristic refers to informal, experience-based strategies or mental shortcuts used to make quick, approximate judgments or decisions when exact data or time for deep analysis is unavailable. Rather than following rigorous algorithms or mathematical models, rule-of-thumb estimates rely on general principles or past experiences that have worked reasonably well in similar situations.

These heuristics are widely used in everyday decision-making and professional domains like engineering, medicine, finance, and project management. They trade precision for **speed, efficiency, and cognitive simplicity**, making them especially useful under uncertainty or time pressure.

Example

A common rule-of-thumb in real estate is the "1% rule": if the monthly rent for a property is approximately 1% of its purchase price, it's considered a potentially good investment. So, if a house costs $200,000, you'd expect it to rent for at least $2,000 per month. This estimate doesn't account for all variables—like taxes, vacancies, or maintenance—but offers a quick, reasonable starting point.

Another well-known rule is the "20/4/10" rule in personal finance: spend no more than 20% of your income on car expenses, make a 20% down payment, and finance for no more than 4 years. Again, not precise, but practical.

Why It Works

Rule-of-thumb estimates work because they simplify complex decision-making into **manageable heuristics** based on patterns that tend to hold across similar situations. They function effectively when:

- Precise data is unavailable or difficult to process.

- Speed is more valuable than accuracy.

- The decision-maker has prior experience or learned generalizations.

By leveraging human intuition and experience, these heuristics **reduce cognitive load** and enable quick, actionable outcomes— though they are always subject to some margin of error.

How It Works

1. **Identify a relevant domain** (e.g., budgeting, construction, time management).

2. **Apply a generalized heuristic** drawn from prior experience or conventional wisdom.

3. **Use it to make a decision or estimate** (e.g., time, cost, probability).

4. **Adjust or refine** based on feedback, if necessary.

These heuristics are often taught, passed down, or derived from accumulated domain knowledge and shared industry practices.

Application

Rule-of-thumb estimates are used in:

- **Project management** (e.g., estimating that writing takes 1 hour per 500 words).

- **Engineering** (e.g., assuming material safety factors).

- **Healthcare** (e.g., calculating medication dosages based on weight).

- **Daily life** (e.g., tipping 15–20% at restaurants).

They're especially valuable in early-stage planning, where detailed calculations are premature or impractical.

Key Insights

- Rule-of-thumb estimates enable **fast, intuitive decisions** in uncertain or high-pressure situations.

- They are **not foolproof** but often "good enough" for practical use.

- Their effectiveness depends on **domain knowledge, pattern recognition, and adaptability**.

- They reveal that **approximate answers can outperform perfection** when speed and simplicity are paramount.

In essence, this heuristic reminds us that **sometimes, near-enough is more than enough—especially when the clock is ticking**.

39. Branch and bound heuristic

Branch and Bound is a problem-solving heuristic and algorithmic framework used for **combinatorial and discrete optimization problems**, particularly when the goal is to find the best solution among many possible configurations. It systematically explores the solution space by dividing it into smaller subproblems (*branching*) and uses **upper and lower bounds** to eliminate paths (*bounding*) that cannot lead to an optimal solution. This allows for an **intelligent pruning of the search tree**, making the approach significantly more efficient than brute-force methods.

Unlike greedy algorithms, which make decisions based on local information, Branch and Bound is an **exhaustive yet selective** search strategy that guarantees optimality—provided it is given enough time and appropriate bounding logic.

Example

Consider the **Traveling Salesman Problem (TSP)**, where a salesperson must visit each city exactly once and return to the starting point, minimizing total travel distance. Using Branch and Bound:

- The algorithm starts with a partial path.

- It estimates a lower bound on the shortest route that can be completed from that partial path.

- If the lower bound is worse than a known complete solution, it discards that branch.

- Otherwise, it further branches into extended paths, repeating the process.

This allows the algorithm to **skip entire subtrees** of possibilities that cannot outperform the current best solution.

Why It Works

Branch and Bound works because it combines **systematic enumeration** with **smart elimination**. The bounding mechanism enables the algorithm to focus only on promising regions of the solution space while discarding poor prospects early. This saves computational time and resources, especially when the problem space grows exponentially (as in TSP, knapsack, or integer programming problems).

The method is especially powerful when the bounding function is tight (i.e., accurately predicts the minimum or maximum possible cost), which enables **aggressive pruning**.

How It Works

1. **Initialize**: Start with an initial solution or upper bound (best-known value).

2. **Branch**: Divide the current problem into smaller subproblems (subsets of the solution space).

3. **Bound**: Estimate the best possible solution (lower or upper bound) within each subproblem.

4. **Prune**: Discard subproblems that cannot outperform the current best solution.

5. **Repeat**: Explore the remaining branches until all are either solved or pruned.

The process can be visualized as navigating a decision tree, where nodes represent partial solutions.

Application

Branch and Bound is used in:

- **Operations research** (e.g., scheduling, assignment problems)

- **Logistics and route planning**

- **Knapsack and bin-packing problems**

- **Integer and linear programming**

- **Game theory** and **puzzle solving** (e.g., solving Sudoku optimally)

It's especially valuable in **NP-hard problems**, where complete enumeration is computationally infeasible.

Key Insights

- Branch and Bound guarantees optimality while minimizing unnecessary computation.

- Its efficiency depends heavily on the **quality of bounds** and **pruning criteria**.

- It is both **exhaustive and strategic**, balancing completeness with performance.

- The approach reflects a broader principle: **knowing what not to solve is as important as solving well**.

In essence, Branch and Bound illustrates how **structure, estimation, and smart decisions** can transform exhaustive search into a tractable and powerful optimization tool.

40. Upper/lower bound estimation heuristic

The *Upper/Lower Bound Estimation* heuristic is a problem-solving and optimization strategy used to define the **best-possible limits** within which the actual solution to a problem must lie. A **lower bound** is an estimate of the minimum achievable value (e.g., cost, distance, time), while an **upper bound** is an estimate of the maximum. These bounds help guide search, decision-making, and pruning by identifying **how close a candidate solution is to optimality**, or whether further exploration is worthwhile.

This heuristic plays a central role in optimization algorithms such as **branch and bound**, **cutting planes**, **approximation schemes**, and **integer programming**, where it is crucial to efficiently limit the solution space.

Example

In the **Traveling Salesman Problem (TSP)**, suppose you're trying to determine the shortest route visiting several cities. You might start by computing a **lower bound**: for instance, summing the shortest distance from each city to any other unvisited city. This doesn't give you the exact shortest path, but it tells you that no valid tour can be shorter than this.

Simultaneously, you may construct a quick complete tour using a heuristic like **nearest neighbour**—yielding an **upper bound**. The true optimal solution, therefore, must lie somewhere between the lower and upper bounds. This interval helps assess whether continuing the search is worthwhile or if an existing solution is "good enough."

Why It Works

Bound estimation works because it introduces **structured guidance** into potentially unmanageable search spaces. When bounds are tight (i.e., close to the actual optimal value), they provide powerful decision-making information. For example:

- If the **lower bound exceeds the best-known solution**, further exploration can be pruned.

- If the **gap between upper and lower bounds is small**, the current solution is near-optimal.

This heuristic prevents exhaustive exploration and focuses resources where they are most needed.

How It Works

1. **Define an estimation strategy**: Use a relaxed version of the problem or historical data to compute the bounds.

2. **Calculate lower bound**: Determine the minimum possible outcome (e.g., relaxed constraints or linear approximations).

3. **Calculate upper bound**: Use heuristics or greedy algorithms to get a feasible (not necessarily optimal) solution.

4. **Compare and update**: Use bounds to guide decisions (prune branches, accept near-optimal solutions, or continue refining).

As the search progresses, these bounds are continuously updated to reflect new information.

Application

Upper/lower bound estimation is widely used in:

- **Combinatorial optimization** (TSP, knapsack problem)

- **Project scheduling** and **resource allocation**

- **Machine learning** (e.g., bounding error in model training)

- **Operations research**, especially with **integer or linear programming**

Key Insights

- Upper/lower bound estimation enhances **efficiency, direction, and clarity** in problem-solving.

- The tighter the bounds, the faster a solution can be confirmed or improved.

- It allows **early stopping** when further refinement would not change the outcome meaningfully.

- It shows that **knowing what's impossible or sufficient** is often as valuable as finding what's optimal.

In essence, this heuristic reflects the idea that **setting smart limits helps make better, faster decisions under complexity and uncertainty**.

💻 **Economic & Behavioural Heuristics**

41. Endowment effect heuristic

The *Endowment Effect* is a psychological heuristic wherein individuals place a higher value on items they own simply because they own them. This valuation bias leads people to demand more money to give something up than they would be willing to pay to acquire the same item. It's a form of **loss aversion**, closely tied to prospect theory, and was first formally identified by economists Richard Thaler, Daniel Kahneman, and Jack Knetsch.

Unlike rational economic models that assume people's valuation of a good is independent of ownership, the endowment effect suggests that **ownership creates emotional or cognitive attachment**, altering perceived value. It is not just limited to physical possessions but also applies to ideas, rights, status, or even default choices.

Example

In a famous experiment, participants were randomly given either a mug or a chocolate bar. Later, they were offered a chance to trade. Theoretically, about 50% should have switched if preferences were symmetrical. However, the majority chose to **keep what they were given**, indicating that merely owning the item increased its perceived worth.

In another example, homeowners often **overprice their property** because they focus on personal memories and perceived value, ignoring objective market data. Buyers, however, don't share this emotional investment and are less willing to pay inflated prices.

Why It Works

The endowment effect works because humans are naturally **loss-averse**: the pain of losing something is psychologically more significant than the pleasure of gaining something of equal value. Ownership shifts an item's status from a potential gain to a potential loss, which activates this aversion.

Additionally, **identity and attachment** play roles. People often incorporate possessions into their sense of self, making parting with them feel like a personal loss.

How It Works

1. **Ownership Establishment**: An individual comes to possess or control an item.

2. **Value Inflation**: Ownership increases the perceived value of the item beyond market norms.

3. **Decision Impact**: When considering selling or trading, the perceived loss looms larger than potential gains.

4. **Resistance to Exchange**: The person hesitates or refuses to part with the item unless compensated significantly beyond its objective value.

This process often occurs unconsciously and affects both individuals and institutions.

Application

The endowment effect influences:

- **Marketing and pricing**: Free trials and samples create ownership-like feelings, increasing purchase likelihood.

- **Negotiation**: Sellers anchor to inflated prices due to perceived loss in parting.

- **Behavioural economics**: Explains inefficiencies in trading, investment holding biases, and resistance to policy changes.

- **Legal disputes**: Parties may overvalue entitlements simply because they hold them.

Key Insights

- The endowment effect reveals that **perceived value is not fixed**—it is shaped by ownership and emotion.

- It contributes to **status quo bias**, anchoring, and reluctance to change.

- Understanding it can help mitigate overpricing, negotiation stalemates, and irrational decision-making.

- It shows that **what we own changes how we think**, not just what we do.

In essence, the endowment effect reminds us that **possession transforms perception—and not always rationally**.

42. Price-quality heuristic

The *Price-Quality Heuristic* is a cognitive shortcut where individuals infer the quality of a product or service based on its price. In the absence of complete information, consumers often assume that **"you get what you pay for"**—that higher prices indicate superior quality, reliability, or performance. This heuristic simplifies decision-making under uncertainty and is especially prevalent in markets where evaluating product quality directly is difficult or time-consuming.

Rooted in both **consumer psychology** and **behavioural economics**, the price-quality heuristic allows buyers to resolve ambiguity by using price as a proxy for other, less visible attributes such as durability, brand value, or social prestige.

Example

Consider a consumer shopping for wine without deep knowledge of wine labels, regions, or production methods. Faced with ten bottles ranging in price from $7 to $45, the consumer might reason that the $30 bottle is better than the $12 one, not because of a taste test or review, but because its price suggests greater craftsmanship, refinement, or brand status.

This heuristic is also observed in healthcare: patients may judge a more expensive medical procedure or private hospital visit as inherently better than a cheaper, equally effective public option, simply due to perceived cost-related value.

Why It Works

The price-quality heuristic works because price is **salient, easily understood**, and often **correlates with quality**—but not always. In many markets, especially where quality is difficult to observe or assess (e.g., fashion, electronics, specialty foods), price serves as an accessible stand-in for deeper evaluation.

From an evolutionary standpoint, humans have developed sensitivity to cost as a signal of effort or scarcity. Psychologically, **expensive items trigger perceptions of exclusivity, reliability, or luxury**, enhancing their perceived utility.

How It Works

1. **Encounter a decision under uncertainty** (e.g., choosing between unknown products).

2. **Use price as a heuristic cue** in lieu of direct product information.

3. **Infer quality level**: higher price → higher quality, and vice versa.

4. **Make purchasing or evaluation decision** based on inferred value.

This process is often subconscious and reinforced by marketing, packaging, and brand messaging.

Application

The price-quality heuristic is widely used in:

- **Marketing and branding**: Luxury goods and services are priced higher to signal premium quality.

- **Consumer behaviour**: Buyers often choose mid- or high-priced options assuming better performance or longevity.

- **E-commerce**: In product listings without reviews, consumers often default to higher-priced options.

- **Healthcare and education**: Patients and students may associate higher cost with better treatment or instruction.

Key Insights

- The heuristic offers **speed and simplicity**, reducing the burden of complex decision-making.

- It is **not always accurate**; high price doesn't guarantee high quality.

- Marketers often **manipulate perceived value** through pricing strategies.

- Consumers using this heuristic should seek **objective product information** when possible.

In essence, the price-quality heuristic reveals that **perceived value often rides on the price tag—not just the product itself**.

43. Scarcity heuristic

The *Scarcity Heuristic* is a mental shortcut where people assign greater value to items, opportunities, or information that appear to be scarce or limited in availability. This cognitive bias operates on the principle that **rarity implies worth**—if something is difficult to obtain, it must be valuable. Rooted in evolutionary psychology and economic theory, the scarcity heuristic helps individuals prioritize resources under uncertainty or competition by interpreting limited availability as a signal of quality, demand, or future unavailability.

This heuristic is often **automatic and emotionally charged**, triggering urgency, fear of missing out (FOMO), and competitive behaviour. It's a cornerstone of marketing tactics and behavioural influence strategies.

Example

Imagine browsing a travel website and seeing a notice: "Only 2 rooms left at this price!" Although you might not have intended to book immediately, the urgency created by limited supply increases the likelihood of acting quickly. Even without full evaluation of the room's features, the perceived scarcity increases its attractiveness.

Another example is the popularity of limited-edition sneakers. When a brand releases a new pair in small quantities, demand often skyrockets—not necessarily due to the shoe's performance or comfort, but because the rarity amplifies its desirability and perceived status value.

Why It Works

The scarcity heuristic works because humans evolved in environments where resources were genuinely limited. Prioritizing rare opportunities—whether food, shelter, or mates—was advantageous for survival. In modern contexts, this bias persists: we equate **scarcity with opportunity**, viewing rare items as more valuable or urgent.

It also taps into **social proof**: if something is scarce, it might be because others want it. This compounds the perceived value, even if we lack independent information about its quality.

How It Works

1. **Encounter limited availability**: A product, offer, or opportunity appears scarce (e.g., "last in stock").

2. **Trigger emotional urgency**: The individual feels pressure to act to avoid missing out.

3. **Infer high value**: Scarcity is interpreted as an indicator of quality, demand, or uniqueness.

4. **Decision influenced**: The scarcity shifts the decision-making process from rational evaluation to impulse or urgency-based action.

This often bypasses slower, analytical thinking in favour of fast, intuitive judgment.

Application

The scarcity heuristic is heavily applied in:

5. **Marketing and e-commerce**: "Only 3 left!", "Limited-time offer," or "While supplies last."

6. **Event ticketing**: Early-bird deals or exclusive access windows increase early conversion.

7. **Product launches**: Limited editions or flash sales drive hype and urgency.

8. **Social dynamics**: Exclusive memberships or invite-only apps (e.g., early Clubhouse) gain popularity partly due to limited access.

Key Insights

- Scarcity can **artificially inflate perceived value**, leading to impulsive or suboptimal decisions.

- It leverages **emotion over logic**, creating urgency without always justifying it.

- While effective for businesses, overuse can lead to **consumer distrust**.

- Being aware of this heuristic helps individuals make **more deliberate, informed choices**.

In essence, the scarcity heuristic reminds us that **when something is rare, we rush to value it—but sometimes, that rush should be questioned.**

44. Social proof heuristic

The *Social Proof Heuristic* is a cognitive shortcut where individuals determine what is correct or desirable by observing the behaviours and decisions of others. In uncertain or ambiguous situations, people look to the actions of the majority—or those perceived as similar or authoritative—as evidence of the "right" behaviour. This heuristic is rooted in **social psychology**, particularly the work of Robert Cialdini, and explains how human behaviour is shaped by perceived norms, especially in unfamiliar or high-stakes environments.

The fundamental assumption behind this heuristic is that **if many people are doing something, it must be good, correct, or worthwhile**. It serves as a social validation mechanism and plays a major role in both everyday decision-making and collective human behaviour.

Example

Consider someone choosing a restaurant in a new city. They come across two side-by-side options: one is busy and filled with diners, while the other is nearly empty. Even without knowing anything about the food quality, the person is more likely to choose the busier restaurant. The visible presence of other people is interpreted as a signal that the place is popular, and therefore, likely better.

This effect is also seen in online shopping. A product with thousands of positive reviews or labelled as a "best seller" often draws more purchases, regardless of actual specifications, because buyers are influenced by what others are doing.

Why It Works

The social proof heuristic works because human beings are **inherently social creatures** who evolved in groups. Mimicking the behaviour of others was often a low-risk survival strategy—if most people avoided a certain food or path, it was likely unsafe. In modern settings, the same principle persists: in situations of uncertainty, we defer to collective behaviour as a safe guide.

Social proof also offers **efficiency**. Instead of investing time and cognitive effort in evaluating every option, we rely on the assumption that others have already done the vetting.

How It Works

1. **Encounter a decision under uncertainty**.

2. **Observe others' actions or endorsements**.

3. **Infer correctness or value** based on observed behaviour.

4. **Conform decision-making** to the group's choice.

This process can be conscious (e.g., reading reviews) or subconscious (e.g., following a crowd in an emergency).

Application

The social proof heuristic is widely applied in:

- **Marketing**: Customer testimonials, star ratings, "most popular" tags.

- **Digital platforms**: Likes, shares, and follower counts influence credibility.

- **Social influence**: Public health campaigns showing community participation.

- **Consumer behaviour**: "People who bought this also bought..." prompts.

Key Insights

- Social proof simplifies decisions in complex or unfamiliar situations.

- It is powerful but **can lead to herd behaviour**, reinforcing bad choices or misinformation.

- **Perceived similarity** increases influence—people trust the behaviour of those like themselves.

- Social proof is a **double-edged sword**: it can inform or manipulate.

In essence, the social proof heuristic reflects our deep-rooted belief that **there's safety in numbers—even when we don't fully understand the crowd.**

45. Heuristic value estimation

Heuristic Value Estimation is a decision-making strategy in which individuals or systems assign approximate values to options or outcomes based on simplified rules or incomplete information, rather than calculating exact values. This heuristic is especially useful in complex environments where exhaustive analysis is either impractical or impossible due to time, cognitive, or computational constraints.

The goal of heuristic value estimation is not to find the precise, mathematically optimal choice, but rather to produce a **"good enough" approximation** that supports timely and efficient decision-making. It is widely used in **artificial intelligence**, **economics**, and **human cognition**, especially when evaluating potential actions in uncertain or dynamic environments.

Example

In chess-playing AI, heuristic value estimation is used to evaluate board positions. The program assigns point values to pieces (e.g., 9 for a queen, 5 for a rook, 3 for a bishop or knight, 1 for a pawn) and factors in positioning, control of space, and king safety. These values guide decision-making without exploring every possible outcome to the end of the game.

For humans, consider job offers: someone may estimate the overall value of an offer by combining approximate weights for salary, commute, flexibility, and company reputation. Even if the evaluation isn't exact, it's sufficient to guide a decision without spreadsheets or formal models.

Why It Works

This heuristic works because in many real-world scenarios, **precise calculations are either infeasible or unnecessary**. The mind (or a machine) benefits from a rough approximation that guides action without getting bogged down by computational cost. Heuristic value estimation is particularly effective when:

- The structure of the problem allows for informative simplifications.

- Resources (time, cognitive bandwidth) are limited.

- A perfect answer is less important than a timely one.

It also mimics how people make decisions intuitively—using past experience, pattern recognition, and relative comparisons rather than strict computation.

How It Works

1. **Define key attributes** of the decision context (e.g., cost, benefit, risk).

2. **Assign estimated values** based on experience, rules of thumb, or simplified models.

3. **Combine or compare values** to make a judgment or select the best option.

4. **Refine estimates** over time through feedback or learning.

Heuristic estimators may be based on linear models, lookup tables, or subjective ratings.

Application

Heuristic value estimation is used in:

- **AI search algorithms** (e.g., A* and minimax with evaluation functions).

- **Economics and behavioural finance** (e.g., how consumers estimate the value of complex bundles).

- **Everyday human decisions** (e.g., choosing a home, evaluating risks, or planning routes).

- **Robotics and real-time systems**, where speed is critical.

Key Insights

- Heuristic value estimation allows **fast, flexible, and adaptive decisions** in uncertain or complex environments.

- It trades **accuracy for efficiency**, often with minimal performance loss.

- It reflects how both machines and humans handle real-world ambiguity using **estimation, not precision**.

- Proper calibration is key: **bad heuristics lead to systematic errors**, while good ones guide near-optimal choices.

In essence, heuristic value estimation teaches that **"good enough" decisions made quickly often outperform perfect ones made too late**.

46. Compromise effect heuristic

The *Compromise Effect* is a decision-making heuristic observed when individuals are more likely to choose an option that represents a **middle ground** among available alternatives, rather than the extremes. This effect stems from people's tendency to avoid the perceived risk of the highest or lowest option, opting instead for a choice that feels "safe," "reasonable," or "balanced." It is widely recognized in **behavioural economics** and **consumer psychology**, particularly in contexts involving product choice, pricing, and feature differentiation.

The compromise effect is linked to **context-dependent preferences**, meaning a person's valuation of an option depends on how it compares to other available alternatives. It reveals that choices are not made in a vacuum, but rather in relation to how other options frame them.

Example

Imagine a consumer shopping for a new coffee machine and confronted with three options:

- **Basic Model**: $80, few features

- **Mid-Range Model**: $150, more features

- **Premium Model**: $280, full features

Even if the consumer initially planned to spend less, they may end up selecting the mid-range model—not because it is necessarily the best value or best quality, but because it appears to be a **compromise** between affordability and performance. The presence of the premium option makes the mid-range model seem more reasonable by comparison.

This effect is often engineered by marketers who add a high-end product not to sell it, but to **nudge consumers toward the mid-priced item**.

Why It Works

The compromise effect works due to two key psychological forces:

1. **Risk aversion**: People tend to avoid extremes, which feel riskier—too cheap may signal low quality, too expensive may seem excessive.

2. **Justifiability**: Middle options are easier to rationalize and defend, especially in social or shared decision contexts.

It aligns with the **heuristic of satisficing**—choosing an option that is "good enough" rather than perfect—by providing a perceived balance.

How It Works

1. **Introduce three or more options** with varying prices and features.

2. **Frame the middle option** to contrast against an expensive and a basic alternative.

3. **Trigger consumer psychology**: the moderate choice feels both safe and sensible.

4. **Increase selection likelihood** of the compromise item.

This effect often disappears or weakens when only two options are presented, as the reference frame becomes less defined.

Application

The compromise effect is used in:

- **Retail pricing**: Offering three-tier packages to increase mid-tier sales.

- **Service plans**: Phone, insurance, and streaming services structure choices to drive toward the "reasonable middle."

- **Product design**: Configuring "decoy" options to influence the perceived value of a target choice.

- **Behavioural interventions**: Nudging healthier or safer choices by making them appear moderate.

Key Insights

- Consumers' preferences are **context-sensitive**, not fixed.

- The compromise effect reveals how **choice architecture** shapes behaviour.

- It challenges rational choice theory by showing decisions aren't solely based on absolute preferences.

- This heuristic highlights the power of **perceived balance and justifiability** in decision-making.

In essence, the compromise effect reminds us that **what feels like a rational decision is often the result of carefully structured context**.

47. Default bias heuristic

Default Bias—also known as **status quo bias**—is a cognitive heuristic where individuals tend to **stick with pre-set or existing options** rather than actively choosing alternatives. It reflects a preference for inaction over action when a default option is presented, often because changing the default requires effort, introduces uncertainty, or evokes the fear of making a wrong decision. This bias is rooted in **behavioural economics** and **decision science**, and is widely leveraged in policy design, marketing, and user experience (UX).

At its core, default bias reflects human tendencies toward **cognitive laziness**, **loss aversion**, and **inertia**. People are more likely to accept what is given by default, especially in complex or low-engagement contexts, even when better alternatives may exist.

Example

One of the most widely cited examples of default bias is in **organ donation systems**. Countries that use an "opt-out" model (where individuals are donors by default unless they actively refuse) have **dramatically higher donation rates** than those with an "opt-in" system. For instance, Austria has a donor consent rate over 90% under an opt-out system, while Germany, with an opt-in model, remains below 15%.

Despite the moral and personal nature of this choice, many individuals do not bother to make an active selection—demonstrating the powerful impact of default framing.

Why It Works

Default bias works due to several psychological mechanisms:

- **Effort avoidance**: People often prefer the path of least resistance, especially when the perceived benefit of change is unclear.

- **Loss aversion**: Changing the default might feel risky or like a potential loss, especially if the current option is working "well enough."

- **Decision paralysis**: In overwhelming or complex situations, sticking with the default provides a cognitive shortcut and reduces decision fatigue.

Additionally, people tend to assume that defaults are **endorsed or recommended** by authorities or experts, further reinforcing compliance.

How It Works

1. **A default option is set**—either explicitly (pre-selected choice) or implicitly (do nothing and this happens).

2. **Individual encounters the choice** but feels little motivation to change it.

3. **No action is taken**, and the default is accepted, often without much deliberation.

4. **Decision becomes sticky**, reinforcing future choices or behaviours in similar contexts.

This process is often unconscious and more pronounced in low-engagement scenarios or under cognitive load.

Application

Default bias is used strategically in:

- **Public policy** (e.g., automatic enrolment in pension plans, organ donation)

- **UX/UI design** (e.g., pre-ticked boxes for newsletters or privacy settings)

- **Health behaviour** (e.g., default prescriptions or treatment paths)

- **E-commerce** (e.g., default shipping methods or tip amounts)

Defaults are powerful "nudges" that steer behaviour while preserving freedom of choice.

Key Insights

- Defaults can significantly shape behaviour without coercion.

- They are especially effective in situations involving **complexity, uncertainty, or low motivation**.

- While helpful for promoting beneficial outcomes, defaults can also be **manipulative** if poorly designed.

- Designing ethical defaults is a **powerful tool in choice architecture**.

In essence, the default bias shows that **the easiest path often becomes the chosen one—not because it's best, but because it's easiest**.

48. Temporal discounting heuristic

Temporal Discounting—also known as **delay discounting**—is a cognitive heuristic where individuals tend to assign **less value to future rewards** compared to immediate ones, even if the future reward is objectively larger. In other words, people disproportionately prefer a smaller, sooner reward over a larger, later one. This heuristic is a key concept in behavioural economics and psychology and plays a central role in impulsivity, self-control, and long-term planning.

Temporal discounting reflects the human tendency to **devalue benefits as the delay to receiving them increases**. It is often modelled mathematically using discount functions (e.g., exponential or hyperbolic), which show how perceived value declines with time.

Example

A classic example involves financial choices. Suppose you're offered $50 today or $80 in a month. Many people choose the $50—even though waiting would yield a 60% return—because the immediate reward feels more tangible and emotionally satisfying. This same bias explains why people may overspend on credit cards, skip saving for retirement, or delay starting healthy habits.

In contrast, someone who applies long-term thinking might recognize the benefit of the delayed reward and opt for the $80, especially if they've developed strategies to manage short-term temptation.

Why It Works

Temporal discounting works because evolution prioritized **immediate survival and gratification**. In uncertain environments, future rewards could be lost to chance, theft, or death. Thus, taking what's available now made adaptive sense.

In modern settings, this legacy of **short-term bias** often leads to suboptimal decisions. The immediacy of reward activates the brain's dopamine system, producing a stronger emotional pull than a distant outcome. The farther away a reward is in time, the more abstract and uncertain it feels—reducing its perceived value.

How It Works

1. **A decision involves trade-offs between present and future outcomes** (e.g., spend vs. save).

2. **The individual assigns lower value to future options**, often unconsciously.

3. **Present-biased choices are favoured**, even at the cost of long-term benefit.

4. **Rationalizations follow**, reinforcing the immediate decision (e.g., "I'll start saving next month").

This process often involves **heuristic shortcuts** that ignore full cost-benefit analysis over time.

Application

Temporal discounting is observed in:

- **Health behaviour**: Choosing junk food over dieting, skipping exercise.

- **Finance**: Undersaving for retirement, impulsive spending.

- **Addiction**: Preference for immediate highs over long-term well-being.

- **Public policy**: Difficulty in mobilizing support for climate change or infrastructure investments with delayed benefits.

Interventions such as **commitment devices, framing future rewards more vividly, or using default savings plans** help counteract this bias.

Key Insights

- Temporal discounting reveals how **immediacy dominates decision-making**, even irrationally.

- It's a core obstacle to **self-control, long-term planning, and delayed gratification**.

- The effect is stronger under **stress, cognitive load, or low self-regulation**.

- Designing for the future requires structuring environments that **make delayed rewards more tangible and accessible**.

In essence, the temporal discounting heuristic shows that **today often wins—not because it's better, but because it's now**.

49. Decoy effect heuristic

The *Decoy Effect*—also known as **asymmetric dominance**—is a cognitive bias and decision-making heuristic where people's preferences between two options change when a third, less attractive (decoy) option is introduced. The decoy is deliberately crafted to be **clearly inferior** to one of the original options but not to the other, making the target option look more attractive by comparison.

This heuristic demonstrates that **preferences are not fixed or absolute**; instead, they can be manipulated by how options are framed and compared. The decoy effect challenges classical economic models of rational choice, which assume consistent preferences independent of context.

Example

Consider this set of subscription options for a magazine:

- **Option A**: Online-only subscription – $59

- **Option B**: Print + online subscription – $125

- **Option C (Decoy)**: Print-only subscription – $125

In studies by behavioural economist Dan Ariely, most people initially preferred the cheaper online-only option (A). But when the print-only decoy (C) was introduced, making Option B look like a better deal (same price as C but with more value), preference shifted dramatically toward Option B. The decoy (C) was rarely chosen but made Option B appear superior through comparison.

Why It Works

The decoy effect works because people often rely on **relative comparisons** when making choices. When facing complex or uncertain decisions, individuals look for shortcuts—like comparing features and prices side by side. The decoy provides a reference point that **skews perception**, making one option seem like a clearly better value.

It exploits the **contrast effect**: the presence of a clearly inferior choice magnifies the appeal of the dominant option. The mind interprets the difference as meaningful, even if the decoy wasn't a real consideration.

How It Works

1. **Present two initial options** that vary in price or features.

2. **Introduce a third decoy option** that is clearly worse than one of the two (but similar).

3. **Trigger relative evaluation**: people compare the decoy with the similar but better option.

4. **Shift preference toward the dominant option**, as it now seems like the best value.

This manipulation subtly nudges the decision without limiting freedom of choice.

Application

The decoy effect is frequently used in:

- **Marketing and pricing strategy**: upselling mid-tier products or services.

- **Menu design**: adding expensive "anchor" items to make other items seem reasonable.

- **E-commerce**: displaying irrelevant but similar alternatives to influence buying behaviour.

- **Public policy or surveys**: influencing responses by adding skewed options.

Key Insights

- The decoy effect shows that **context matters deeply in decision-making**.

- Preferences can be **predictably shaped**, even without deception.

- It highlights how humans use **comparison, not absolute reasoning**, to judge value.

- Effective use of decoys can ethically guide decisions—but misuse risks manipulation.

In essence, the decoy effect reveals that **we often don't choose what's best—we choose what looks best next to something worse**.

50. Habit-based heuristics

Habit-based heuristics are cognitive shortcuts where decisions are guided not by fresh deliberation or analysis, but by **previously learned behaviours** that have been repeated enough to become automatic. When a person encounters a familiar context or decision, rather than weighing options each time, they rely on an ingrained behavioural response formed from past reinforcement. These habits reduce cognitive effort and support efficiency, especially in routine or low-stakes situations.

This heuristic intersects with behavioural psychology and neuroscience, showing how **the brain favors energy-saving mechanisms**, reinforcing behaviours that have worked in the past—whether optimal or not. Unlike purely rational models of decision-making, habit-based heuristics emphasize **consistency over computation**.

Example

Consider your morning routine: you might automatically reach for the same brand of toothpaste, follow the same order of steps (shower, coffee, email), or drive the same route to work—even if alternative routes or products exist. These choices are often made with **little or no conscious deliberation**, reflecting learned behaviours triggered by context, not fresh evaluation.

Similarly, a consumer may habitually buy the same brand of cereal, not because it's objectively best, but because it's familiar and has always "worked." Even if a superior product is introduced, the default behaviour persists—unless disrupted by a significant event or incentive.

Why It Works

Habit-based heuristics work because they **minimize cognitive load**, allowing the brain to allocate effort to novel or complex tasks. In familiar environments, habits:

- **Speed up decisions**

- **Reduce mental fatigue**

- **Provide psychological comfort** through routine and predictability

Neuroscience supports this with findings that habitual behaviour is largely governed by the **basal ganglia**, which activates when decisions are automatic. In contrast, deliberate reasoning relies more on the prefrontal cortex, which is resource-intensive.

How It Works

1. **Behaviour is repeated** in a stable context (e.g., same store, time, mood).

2. **Positive reinforcement** occurs (e.g., satisfaction, efficiency).

3. The behaviour becomes **automatic**—a heuristic that bypasses active deliberation.

4. **Cues or triggers** (time of day, environment, internal state) prompt the habitual response.

5. The habit continues unless disrupted by a change in context or outcome.

Over time, these shortcuts form default behaviours that feel intuitive and "right," even without conscious thought.

Application

Habit-based heuristics are leveraged in:

- **Consumer behaviour**: Brand loyalty, shopping routines.

- **UX design**: Apps use consistent layouts to reinforce repeat usage.

- **Health interventions**: Habit stacking (e.g., taking medication after brushing teeth).

- **Productivity**: Creating rituals around focus, work, or breaks.

Marketers and designers aim to create environments where **desired behaviours become habits**.

Key Insights

- Habit-based heuristics reflect how **past behaviour shapes future decisions**.

- They offer **efficiency and predictability**, but can **resist change** even when better alternatives exist.

- Effective behaviour change strategies often target **context cues and repetition** rather than logic.

- Not all habits are beneficial—**awareness is key** to distinguishing helpful from harmful ones.

In essence, habit-based heuristics show that **we often act based on what we've done—not what we've reasoned**.

51. Parsimony (Occam's razor) heuristic

The *Parsimony Heuristic*, commonly referred to as **Occam's Razor**, is a decision-making and problem-solving principle that favors **simpler explanations or solutions** when faced with competing hypotheses. It suggests that, all else being equal, the option with the fewest assumptions should be preferred. Named after the 14th-century philosopher William of Ockham, this heuristic is a cornerstone in philosophy, science, engineering, and everyday reasoning.

Occam's Razor doesn't claim that the simplest solution is always correct—but rather that it's **more likely** to be correct, particularly in the absence of compelling evidence for more complex alternatives. The heuristic reflects the idea that **unnecessary complexity introduces greater room for error**.

Example

Suppose you wake up and find your lawn is wet. Two possible explanations emerge:

1. It rained last night.

2. Your neighbour secretly set up a sprinkler system, turned it on in the middle of the night, and turned it off before you woke up.

While both are technically possible, the **first explanation is simpler**, requiring fewer assumptions. The parsimony heuristic would favour rain as the likelier cause unless additional evidence suggests otherwise.

This logic is often applied in diagnostics—whether medical, mechanical, or psychological—where the goal is to identify the **most plausible explanation** without overcomplicating the issue.

Why It Works

The parsimony heuristic works because simpler models or explanations tend to be:

- **Easier to understand and communicate**

- **Less prone to overfitting** (in statistical models)

- **More testable and falsifiable**

- **Less dependent on uncertain or unverifiable assumptions**

In practical terms, simplicity leads to **efficiency**, reducing cognitive and computational load while improving clarity. It also helps prevent confirmation bias by discouraging people from weaving elaborate narratives to fit limited evidence.

How It Works

1. **Multiple explanations or models are generated** for a given phenomenon.

2. **Each is evaluated** for complexity, assumptions, and coherence.

3. The **simplest explanation** that accounts for the evidence is selected as the working theory.

4. Complexity is introduced **only if new evidence demands it**.

This heuristic is not rigid; it's a guideline that directs attention to the most elegant solution first—then expands as needed.

Application

Parsimony is applied in:

- **Scientific theory building**: Choosing between competing models or hypotheses.

- **Software engineering**: Keeping code or system design simple to reduce bugs and enhance maintainability.

- **AI and machine learning**: Avoiding overfitting by penalizing model complexity (e.g., regularization).

- **Forensics and law**: Evaluating scenarios based on likelihood and simplicity.

Key Insights

- Parsimony helps **cut through noise and distraction**, focusing attention on core elements.

- It promotes **clarity, falsifiability, and testability** in thinking.

- Simpler explanations are often **more robust** in uncertain or incomplete data environments.

- However, parsimony is not a guarantee of truth—**it's a guiding principle, not a proof**.

In essence, the parsimony heuristic reminds us that **the simplest answer is often the best place to start—even in a complex world**.

52. Causal heuristic

The *Causal Heuristic* is a mental shortcut used to make quick judgments by assuming **causal relationships between events**, often without sufficient evidence. Instead of systematically analyzing data or controlling for confounding variables, individuals intuitively connect events based on **proximity, pattern, or prior belief**, inferring that one event causes another. This heuristic reflects our cognitive tendency to seek order and explanation in the world, especially under uncertainty.

While it can lead to effective and adaptive reasoning in many real-life scenarios, it can also give rise to **illusory correlations**, superstitions, or mistaken cause-effect assumptions. Despite its flaws, the causal heuristic serves a practical purpose: it **reduces cognitive effort** by providing immediate, though sometimes inaccurate, explanations for complex phenomena.

Example

Imagine someone who takes a specific vitamin daily and notices they haven't caught a cold all winter. They may conclude, "This vitamin prevents colds," without considering other factors like reduced exposure, improved sleep, or coincidence. The assumption that taking the vitamin caused the lack of illness is a classic use of the causal heuristic.

Similarly, a manager might believe that productivity increased because they implemented a new policy—when the improvement might actually be due to unrelated seasonal trends or team dynamics.

Why It Works

The causal heuristic works because human cognition is **wired for pattern recognition** and **cause-seeking**. In evolutionary terms, detecting cause-effect relationships (e.g., "eating this berry made me sick") had survival value. As a result, the mind is biased toward seeing **agency, intention, and consequence** even when they don't exist.

This heuristic also functions as a **narrative tool**: people prefer coherent, causal explanations over randomness. The brain feels more satisfied and less anxious when it can assign a cause to events, even if the explanation is flawed.

How It Works

1. **Two events occur in sequence** or appear correlated.

2. The mind **infers a causal relationship**, often automatically.

3. The assumption is **reinforced by repeated experience**, anecdotes, or confirmation bias.

4. The causal link becomes a **mental shortcut** for decision-making or prediction.

Once a causal assumption is formed, people often resist revising it, even in light of contradictory evidence.

Application

The causal heuristic is common in:

- **Medical beliefs** (e.g., attributing recovery to a specific treatment, ignoring placebo or natural healing).

- **Marketing** (e.g., "using this product improved my energy!").

- **Policy-making** (e.g., linking an intervention to social change without full evaluation).

- **Personal behaviour** (e.g., rituals or habits believed to bring luck or success).

It is also leveraged in **advertising** and **persuasion**, where implied causality influences consumer decisions.

Key Insights

- The causal heuristic simplifies complexity but risks **false conclusions**.

- It's often activated under **uncertainty, time pressure, or emotional salience**.

- Recognizing this heuristic helps in **critical thinking, science, and data analysis**.

- While not always accurate, it reflects an **adaptive bias** that allows for fast, often useful reasoning in daily life.

In essence, the causal heuristic shows that **our minds crave explanation—even when the evidence doesn't demand one**.

53. Base rate neglect heuristic

Base Rate Neglect is a cognitive heuristic in which individuals **ignore or underweight general statistical information** (base rates) in favour of more specific, anecdotal, or vivid information when making judgments. Instead of properly integrating base rates with case-specific evidence, people give disproportionate weight to the details of a story, appearance, or behaviour—even when the base rate should significantly influence the outcome.

This heuristic often leads to **systematic errors in probabilistic reasoning**, and has been extensively studied in psychology by scholars like Daniel Kahneman and Amos Tversky. It highlights a gap between intuitive judgment and normative statistical reasoning.

Example

A classic example involves a personality description:
"Tom is quiet, organized, and detail-oriented. He enjoys working alone and has a preference for structured environments."

Now, asked whether Tom is more likely to be a librarian or a farmer, most people answer "librarian" based on the description. However, if told that there are 20 times more farmers than librarians in the population, the statistically correct answer is that Tom is **more likely** a farmer. The **base rate** (the population proportion) is overlooked in favour of the description, which fits the **stereotype** of a librarian.

Why It Works

Base rate neglect works (or rather misleads) because our minds are better tuned to **narratives, imagery, and specific examples** than to abstract numbers or probabilities. Evolutionarily, this made sense: concrete, immediate cues (like the behaviour of an animal) were more actionable than long-term statistics. As a result, humans are **cognitively biased** to favour salient, personal, or emotionally engaging information.

It also reflects **representativeness bias**—we tend to match an individual case to a category without adjusting for how common or rare that category is.

How It Works

1. **Receive a description or scenario** (specific, vivid information).

2. **Overweight the case-specific detail**, which feels more informative or diagnostic.

3. **Underweight or ignore the base rate**, even when it's relevant or explicitly given.

4. **Form judgment** based on how well the specifics match a stereotype, rather than probability.

This happens unconsciously and often persists even when people are trained in statistics.

Application

Base rate neglect appears in:

- **Medical diagnosis**: Doctors may overweight symptoms and ignore prevalence rates.

- **Legal reasoning**: Jurors may misjudge probabilities of guilt by focusing on the story.

- **Hiring decisions**: Managers focus on personality traits, not prior success rates of similar candidates.

- **Public perception**: People may fear rare events (e.g., plane crashes) due to vivid news, ignoring statistical rarity.

Key Insights

- Base rate neglect shows a **conflict between intuitive and statistical reasoning**.

- It contributes to **biased judgments**, even among trained professionals.

- Correcting it requires explicit integration of statistical reasoning (e.g., using Bayesian approaches).

- Awareness of base rates improves decision quality in uncertain, probabilistic environments.

In essence, this heuristic reminds us that **stories are compelling—but statistics are grounding**.

54. Confirmation bias heuristic

Confirmation Bias is a cognitive heuristic where individuals tend to **seek, interpret, and remember information** in ways that confirm their existing beliefs, hypotheses, or expectations. Rather than impartially evaluating evidence, people give greater weight to supportive data while discounting or ignoring contradictory information. It is a deeply ingrained cognitive shortcut that shapes how we process the world, often **without conscious awareness**.

This heuristic is not simply a flaw in reasoning—it is an **adaptive mechanism** that reduces cognitive dissonance and simplifies information processing. However, it can also reinforce **misconceptions, stereotypes, and poor decision-making**, especially in high-stakes or emotionally charged contexts.

Example

Imagine a person who believes that left-handed people are more creative. When they meet a creative left-handed person, they highlight this as evidence for their belief. When they meet a creative right-handed person, they may dismiss it as an exception. Over time, they build a mental catalogue that **selectively supports their belief**, even if overall evidence does not.

In another example, a political conservative might seek news from right-leaning outlets, reinforcing their views, while ignoring reports from opposing sources. The same holds true in reverse for liberal-leaning individuals. This self-reinforcing loop is a hallmark of confirmation bias.

Why It Works

Confirmation bias works because it supports **cognitive efficiency and emotional comfort**. Evaluating contradictory information requires mental effort and can threaten one's sense of identity, worldview, or social belonging. The mind favors **consistency and coherence**—and confirmation bias preserves that.

It also reduces **decision fatigue** in complex environments by filtering out dissonant information. From an evolutionary perspective, sticking with previously useful beliefs may have helped guide fast action, even at the expense of accuracy.

How It Works

1. **Form an initial belief** based on personal experience, values, or hearsay.

2. **Seek or notice confirming information** more readily than disconfirming data.

3. **Interpret ambiguous evidence** in a way that aligns with existing views.

4. **Remember confirming cases** more vividly or accurately than contrary ones.

5. **Reinforce belief**, creating a self-sustaining cognitive loop.

The bias can affect perception, memory, and reasoning at all stages of thought.

Application

Confirmation bias plays a major role in:

- **Science denial** (e.g., climate change, vaccines)

- **Investing** (e.g., ignoring market warnings that contradict preferred stocks)

- **Hiring decisions** (e.g., focusing on traits that fit preconceived profiles)

- **Medical misdiagnosis** (e.g., sticking to an initial diagnosis despite new symptoms)

It is also foundational in **conspiracy thinking**, echo chambers, and ideological polarization.

Key Insights

- Confirmation bias illustrates how **belief shapes evidence**, rather than the reverse.

- It affects **experts and novices alike**, making it one of the most pervasive cognitive biases.

- Overcoming it requires **conscious effort, exposure to diverse perspectives, and critical thinking** tools like devil's advocacy or Bayesian reasoning.

- Awareness of this heuristic is essential for **rational decision-making and intellectual humility**.

In essence, the confirmation bias heuristic reminds us that **truth-seeking often means confronting what we don't want to believe**.

55. Availability cascade heuristic

The *Availability Cascade* is a cognitive and social heuristic where repeated exposure to a particular idea or narrative increases its perceived credibility and prevalence—regardless of its factual accuracy. Over time, as more people hear and repeat the claim, it gains **momentum and legitimacy**, creating a feedback loop where familiarity is mistaken for truth. The term was introduced by legal scholar Cass Sunstein and economist Timur Kuran in 1999, highlighting how **public discourse and belief formation** can be shaped less by evidence and more by repetition and social amplification.

This heuristic blends the **availability heuristic**—judging likelihood based on how easily examples come to mind—with **social proof**, in which popularity signals credibility.

Example

Consider the widespread belief that vaccines cause autism. Despite being scientifically disproven, the idea spread rapidly in the early 2000s due to media coverage, celebrity endorsements, and online forums. As the claim was repeated—on talk shows, blogs, and social media—it became more familiar, and thus more "believable" to many. This availability cascade led to real-world consequences, including vaccine hesitancy and public health risks.

Another example is panic buying during crises. When media stories focus heavily on people stockpiling essentials (like toilet paper during COVID-19), it creates the impression of scarcity and urgency, prompting others to follow suit—amplifying the behaviour and belief through repetition.

Why It Works

The availability cascade works because humans are **cognitive misers** who rely on mental shortcuts, and the **ease of recall** often stands in for probability or truth. Additionally, **social validation** plays a powerful role: if "everyone is saying it," we're more likely to believe it's true.

Emotionally charged or dramatic information is particularly sticky. It spreads faster and becomes more memorable, feeding the cycle of repetition and acceptance. Over time, **frequency becomes a substitute for accuracy**.

How It Works

1. A claim is introduced—often vivid, emotional, or sensational.

2. The media or individuals **repeat and share** the claim, increasing exposure.

3. The idea becomes more **mentally available**—easier to recall and more familiar.

4. Familiarity breeds **perceived validity**, prompting further repetition.

5. The claim becomes **mainstream belief**, regardless of its factual basis.

This process can be spontaneous or intentionally manipulated.

Application

The availability cascade plays out in:

- **Media and journalism**: Sensational stories get repeated until they're seen as norms.

- **Public policy**: Emotional events (e.g., crime spikes) can drive overreactions.

- **Social media**: Virality often favors repetition over accuracy.

- **Marketing**: Brands leverage repetition to embed messages and beliefs in consumers.

Key Insights

- The availability cascade shows how **beliefs can form and spread independent of truth**.

- Repetition and emotional salience drive belief more than evidence.

- Cascades are difficult to reverse once established, especially in polarized environments.

- Critical thinking, media literacy, and fact-checking are essential defenses.

In essence, the availability cascade reminds us that **what we hear most isn't always what's real—it's just what's repeated**.

56. Relevance heuristic

The *Relevance Heuristic* is a cognitive shortcut where individuals evaluate the importance, validity, or credibility of information based primarily on how **relevant it seems to their current goal, context, or mental focus**, rather than on its objective quality or completeness. In other words, people are more likely to attend to and act on information that *feels* pertinent, even if it's statistically insignificant or incomplete.

This heuristic is closely tied to theories of **bounded rationality** and **limited attention**. Since cognitive resources are finite, the human mind prioritizes information it deems immediately useful or meaningful, often skipping broader analysis. Relevance becomes a **proxy for value**, especially under time pressure, uncertainty, or cognitive load.

Example

Imagine a person shopping for a laptop. They've recently heard a friend say that "battery life is the most important feature." When browsing options, the shopper zeroes in on laptops with long battery life, ignoring other critical specs like processor speed or storage. Though the best-performing laptop overall might not have the longest battery life, the individual uses battery life as a **relevance filter**, shaping their decision based on what currently feels most important.

Another example is in job interviews: if an interviewer sees a résumé that mentions a shared alma mater, that information may be perceived as highly relevant, subtly influencing their perception of the candidate's competence—even if the school has little to do with job performance.

Why It Works

The relevance heuristic works because it supports **efficiency** in decision-making. In a world saturated with information, people need to quickly identify which data points matter. By tuning into what feels relevant, the brain **reduces cognitive overload** and narrows its focus.

It's also emotionally and socially adaptive. We're more likely to notice, recall, and act on information that **aligns with our current needs, goals, or group norms**. This supports rapid decision-making in dynamic environments but also opens the door to biased judgments.

How It Works

1. A decision or evaluation task is triggered.

2. The mind subconsciously scans for information that **feels aligned** with the task or goal.

3. This "relevant" information is prioritized and weighed more heavily.

4. Irrelevant (but possibly important) data may be ignored or undervalued.

5. A decision is formed based on this filtered information stream.

Relevance is often determined by **contextual cues**, recent experiences, or framing effects.

Application

The relevance heuristic plays a role in:

- **Advertising**: Tailoring messages to current consumer interests to increase impact.

- **Search engines**: Ranking results based on user-defined relevance signals.

- **Legal arguments**: Lawyers emphasize facts most pertinent to the case narrative.

- **Education**: Students engage more when content is connected to their personal lives or future goals.

Key Insights

- Relevance often **trumps accuracy** in real-world decision-making.

- It helps manage attention and focus but can lead to **oversimplified or biased reasoning**.

- Context and framing shape what's perceived as relevant.

- Awareness of the heuristic can improve judgment by prompting broader evaluation.

In essence, the relevance heuristic reflects the brain's instinct to ask: **"Does this matter to me right now?"**—but not always whether it should.

57. Analogy heuristic

The *Analogy Heuristic* is a cognitive strategy where individuals solve unfamiliar problems or make decisions by identifying a **similar situation from the past** and applying its solution to the current context. It is based on the idea that if two problems share underlying structures or relationships, then the solution to one can inform the other. This heuristic is widely used in reasoning, learning, creativity, and problem-solving, especially when explicit rules or formulas are unavailable.

Unlike deductive reasoning, which relies on logical inference from general principles, analogy-based reasoning is **relational and experiential**. It leverages memory and pattern recognition, making it both intuitive and powerful—though it can lead to oversimplifications when surface similarities overshadow deeper differences.

Example

A classic example comes from medicine. Suppose a doctor encounters a rare disease that presents similarly to a known illness. Even if they've never seen this new condition before, they might draw an analogy: "This looks like bacterial meningitis," and treat it accordingly. If the assumption is correct, the patient benefits. If incorrect, it could result in ineffective treatment. The heuristic saves time and effort but carries risk when deeper differences are overlooked.

Another example is seen in business strategy. A company facing market disruption may model its response on how another firm navigated a similar crisis. For instance, Netflix's transition from DVDs to streaming could serve as an analogy for a print media company adapting to digital.

Why It Works

The analogy heuristic works because it **simplifies complex or novel problems** by mapping them onto **familiar experiences**. Humans naturally think in patterns and categories, and analogy provides a way to **bridge known and unknown domains**. It draws on our **episodic memory**, allowing for fast, intuitive decisions based on relational similarities.

In many environments, exact information may be missing, and analogy offers a functional approximation. It also encourages **creative transfer**—seeing how solutions in one domain might apply to another.

How It Works

1. Encounter a novel problem or situation.

2. Search memory for similar past experiences or cases.

3. Identify **structural similarities**, not just superficial ones.

4. Map the known solution onto the new problem.

5. Adapt and apply, adjusting for contextual differences.

The key step is recognizing which elements are **relevant and transferable** across cases.

Application

Analogy heuristics are used in:

- **Education**: Teaching abstract concepts through relatable comparisons.

- **Engineering**: Solving technical issues using principles from nature (biomimicry).

- **Law**: Applying legal precedents to current cases.

- **Innovation**: Transferring models across industries (e.g., ride-sharing applied to logistics).

Key Insights

- Analogies promote **understanding, learning, and creativity**, especially in uncertain domains.

- They are only as effective as the **depth of the similarity**—poor analogies can mislead.

- Encouraging analogical thinking can improve **adaptive problem-solving**.

- The heuristic reveals how humans **connect ideas across contexts** rather than isolating them.

In essence, the analogy heuristic shows that **we often solve the new by remembering the old—shaped by how well we understand the link between them.**

58. Hypothesis matching heuristic

The *Hypothesis Matching* heuristic refers to a decision-making strategy where individuals attempt to interpret new information by matching it to a **pre-existing hypothesis or belief** they already hold. Rather than forming hypotheses based on objective data, people tend to evaluate incoming evidence by checking whether it **confirms or supports what they already expect to be true**. This heuristic is strongly linked to confirmation bias, but it emphasizes the mental process of "fitting the data to the hypothesis" rather than developing the hypothesis from the data.

It is commonly used in **diagnostic reasoning, social judgments, and scientific thinking**, particularly when individuals are under cognitive load, time pressure, or working with incomplete information.

Example

Imagine a doctor who sees a patient with fatigue, weight gain, and depression. Based on recent experience, the doctor suspects hypothyroidism. From that point on, the doctor may frame further evidence—such as sluggish reflexes or dry skin—as confirming the hypothyroidism hypothesis, even if these signs are ambiguous or could point to other conditions (like depression or anemia). Lab results that contradict the diagnosis may be downplayed or reinterpreted.

In everyday life, if someone believes a colleague is lazy, they may selectively attend to any instance of slowness or disengagement, reinforcing their hypothesis—even if that same colleague performs well in many areas.

Why It Works

Hypothesis matching works because the human brain is naturally **goal-oriented and cognitively efficient**. Rather than reevaluating every possibility from scratch, the mind seeks to reduce ambiguity by **anchoring onto an initial hypothesis** and seeking consistency with it. This allows for **faster decision-making**, especially in complex or ambiguous environments.

Additionally, people are motivated to maintain internal coherence. Accepting disconfirming evidence often requires effortful reassessment, which can be uncomfortable or destabilizing.

How It Works

1. A hypothesis is generated—either from past experience, stereotypes, or intuitive reasoning.

2. New information is assessed based on whether it supports the hypothesis.

3. Confirming evidence is accepted readily; disconfirming evidence is ignored, reinterpreted, or dismissed.

4. Confidence in the hypothesis grows, even if it's incorrect or incomplete.

This process tends to **reinforce initial assumptions** rather than revise them, especially when feedback is delayed or unclear.

Application

Hypothesis matching occurs in:

- **Medical and clinical diagnostics**

- **Hiring and performance evaluations**

- **Scientific research and theory development**

- **Social perception and stereotype maintenance**

- **Problem-solving in ambiguous contexts (e.g., troubleshooting technical issues)**

To reduce its downsides, professionals use **structured decision aids**, **checklists**, or **blinded assessments** to limit bias.

Key Insights

- Hypothesis matching increases **decision speed but can compromise accuracy**.

- It shows how people often use data to **justify beliefs**, not challenge them.

- Encouraging **hypothesis testing**—seeking disconfirming evidence—is essential in disciplines like science and medicine.

- Awareness of this heuristic helps improve **critical thinking and diagnostic accuracy**.

In essence, hypothesis matching reminds us that **how we interpret information often depends more on what we expect to see than what is actually there**.

59. Narrative coherence heuristic

The *Narrative Coherence* heuristic refers to the cognitive tendency to judge the **truth, plausibility, or validity of a claim** based on how well it fits into a coherent, emotionally satisfying story. Rather than evaluating information strictly through logic, evidence, or probability, people often assess credibility by how smoothly the pieces of a narrative fit together—how complete, causally connected, and meaningful the account seems.

This heuristic stems from our natural reliance on **stories as cognitive tools**. Humans are storytelling creatures: we make sense of the world through narratives that simplify complexity, explain cause and effect, and offer closure. When a story "makes sense," it feels more **truthful**, even if the underlying facts are flawed or incomplete.

Example

Consider a jury trial where two competing explanations for a crime are presented. One lawyer offers a tight, emotionally compelling story: the defendant had motive, opportunity, and was seen near the scene. The opposing attorney provides scattered forensic evidence suggesting someone else's involvement, but lacks a cohesive narrative. Even if the facts technically favour the second argument, the jury may believe the first—because it **"just feels right."**

Similarly, conspiracy theories often thrive on narrative coherence. A theory that ties together seemingly unrelated events (e.g., government cover-ups, financial institutions, secret meetings) can feel persuasive simply because the story is **compelling and complete**, not because it's supported by verifiable evidence.

Why It Works

The narrative coherence heuristic works because stories are:

- **Easier to understand and remember** than raw data or disjointed facts.

- **Emotionally engaging**, which enhances retention and believability.

- **Structured with cause and effect**, which supports intuitive reasoning.

- **Social tools**, used to transmit values, norms, and cultural knowledge.

From an evolutionary standpoint, storytelling helped early humans **learn from experience**, share survival knowledge, and foster group cohesion. This has wired our brains to trust information embedded in compelling stories.

How It Works

1. Individuals receive a story or explanation for an event or issue.

2. They subconsciously evaluate the story's **internal consistency**, emotional tone, and causal flow.

3. If the story is smooth, complete, and resonates with beliefs or experiences, it is judged as **credible**.

4. Conflicting facts or gaps may be ignored or dismissed if they disrupt the coherence.

This makes people **susceptible to bias**, particularly when coherent stories are emotionally charged or ideologically aligned.

Application

The narrative coherence heuristic is used in:

- **Marketing**: Brand stories that connect emotionally with consumers.

- **Politics**: Campaigns that offer simple explanations for complex issues.

- **Legal arguments**: Framing cases around clear, logical timelines and motives.

- **Journalism and media**: Prioritizing story structure over comprehensive fact inclusion.

Key Insights

- Coherent stories can **overshadow factual accuracy** in human judgment.

- People prefer **clarity over complexity**, even at the cost of truth.

- The heuristic reinforces **confirmation bias**, as we favour stories that fit our worldview.

- Encouraging critical thinking means **questioning how well a story matches evidence—not just how well it flows**.

In essence, narrative coherence shows that **a good story often beats a good argument—unless we're trained to tell the difference**.

60. Salience heuristic

The *Salience Heuristic* is a mental shortcut where people judge the importance, frequency, or likelihood of something based on how much it **stands out in their perception**. When a piece of information is **vivid, emotionally striking, unusual, or highly noticeable**, it becomes more mentally available and is weighted more heavily in decision-making—even if it's statistically rare or objectively less relevant. This heuristic is closely linked to attention, memory, and the availability heuristic, but it emphasizes **what captures focus**, not just what comes easily to mind.

Our brains evolved to prioritize **salient stimuli** in order to quickly identify potential threats, rewards, or changes in the environment. As such, the salience heuristic can be useful—but also misleading in modern settings where salience is often manufactured (e.g., media, advertising, politics).

Example

Imagine watching the news and seeing a vivid report about a plane crash. Though air travel is statistically far safer than driving, the intense imagery and emotional impact of the crash story make flying feel riskier. As a result, you might choose to drive instead—demonstrating how **salient information distorts risk perception**.

Another example is in hiring. If a job candidate has a highly unusual feature (such as a tattoo or an accent), that characteristic may become more salient than their actual qualifications, leading the interviewer to over- or undervalue them based on what's most noticeable rather than most relevant.

Why It Works

The salience heuristic works because it reflects how human attention is **selective and limited**. Salient cues grab our focus and dominate our mental processing, often crowding out subtler but more meaningful data. Evolutionarily, this helped prioritize survival-relevant information (e.g., a predator's movement or a change in the environment).

Additionally, **emotionally charged or visually distinctive** elements are easier to remember, making them more influential when people later recall or judge events.

How It Works

1. An individual is exposed to a range of information or stimuli.

2. A particular element **stands out** due to vividness, novelty, emotion, or contrast.

3. This element becomes **mentally prioritized**, affecting perception and memory.

4. Decisions or judgments are formed with **disproportionate weight** given to the salient item.

This often occurs unconsciously and can persist even when people are aware of the broader context.

Application

The salience heuristic appears in:

- **Advertising**: Bright colours, dramatic music, or emotional appeals draw attention to products.

- **Politics**: Candidates emphasize sensational issues to dominate public discourse.

- **Media coverage**: Unusual crimes or disasters receive more coverage, shaping public fear.

- **Legal settings**: Salient evidence (e.g., graphic photos) can bias juries, even when logically irrelevant.

Key Insights

- The salience heuristic explains why **noteworthy events feel more common or important** than they are.

- It can **skew judgment**, especially in risk assessment and moral reasoning.

- Salience often **overrides statistical reasoning**, leading to distorted perceptions.

- Designing for attention (e.g., in communication, design, or policy) requires **ethical awareness** of how salience affects behaviour.

In essence, this heuristic shows that **what grabs our attention can quietly steer our judgment—even when it's not what matters most**.

61. Straight-line heuristic

The *Straight-Line Heuristic* is a cognitive shortcut where people assume that **trends or progressions will continue in a linear fashion**, projecting the future based on a straight-line extrapolation from the past or present. This heuristic simplifies complex or dynamic patterns by **ignoring fluctuations, turning points, or nonlinear growth**, and instead applying a straightforward mental model: *what has been happening will keep happening at the same rate*.

This heuristic is common in forecasting, reasoning about growth, and decision-making under uncertainty. It emerges from the brain's preference for simplicity and pattern consistency, especially when dealing with incomplete data or limited time.

Example

A classic example occurs in finance. An investor sees a stock price rising steadily over the last six months and assumes that it will **continue rising** at the same rate. Without analyzing market volatility, economic factors, or potential corrections, they base their decisions on a simple, linear trend. If a downturn hits, they are caught off guard, having mistaken a short-term pattern for a permanent trajectory.

Another example is in population growth projections. In the mid-20th century, many predicted that global population would continue growing exponentially forever. These predictions were based on straight-line assumptions, ignoring future changes in birth rates, policy, or technological adaptation.

Why It Works

The straight-line heuristic works because humans are naturally drawn to **order, predictability, and simplicity**. Linear models are cognitively easy to grasp and emotionally reassuring. They eliminate ambiguity by creating clear expectations. When time or data are scarce, this shortcut enables **quick forecasts or judgments** without rigorous analysis.

Moreover, many physical and social processes *do* exhibit linearity over short windows, reinforcing the belief that such projections are valid in the long term—when in fact, they often are not.

How It Works

1. Observe a trend or pattern (e.g., rising sales, growing user base).

2. Assume the **future will follow the same direction and rate**.

3. Extrapolate outcomes based on a **constant slope**.

4. Make decisions or set expectations accordingly.

The brain treats the most **salient, recent, or smooth progression** as a basis for extending into the future, even if deeper analysis would suggest variability or inflection points.

Application

This heuristic is widely observed in:

- **Financial forecasting**: Stock predictions based on recent trends.

- **Urban planning**: Estimating infrastructure needs using linear population growth.

- **Climate discussions**: Misjudging nonlinear tipping points as linear effects.

- **Personal planning**: Assuming consistent progress in weight loss, career advancement, or skill learning.

Key Insights

- The straight-line heuristic simplifies forecasting but can **mislead in dynamic systems**.

- It ignores **nonlinear growth, feedback loops, and saturation effects**.

- Effective decision-making requires knowing when a system **is or isn't linear**.

- Tools like **scenario planning or systems thinking** can help correct this bias.

In essence, the straight-line heuristic reveals our **desire for continuity**—even when reality is full of curves, spikes, and plateaus.

62. Left-hand rule (maze solving) heuristic

The *Left-Hand Rule*, also known as the **Wall-Following Heuristic**, is a simple yet effective method for solving certain types of mazes. The core idea is that if you place your **left hand on the wall** at the maze's entrance and keep it there while walking, you will eventually find your way to the exit—assuming the maze is a **simply connected space** (i.e., all walls are connected, with no isolated sections).

This heuristic is based on consistent **physical orientation** rather than abstract planning. It minimizes the need for memory, maps, or problem-solving logic and instead relies on a mechanical, systematic process. It's an example of **embodied cognition**, where the body's position in space drives the solution.

Example

Consider a person trapped in a hedge maze. Rather than trying to memorize every turn or reason through a map, they apply the Left-Hand Rule: place their left hand on the wall and begin walking forward, always keeping their hand in contact with the wall. Over time, this guarantees they will traverse every corridor and reach the exit—unless the maze has disconnected walls or floating islands, in which case the rule may not succeed.

In digital gaming, characters controlled by AI may use a version of this heuristic to explore dungeons or procedurally generated environments.

Why It Works

The Left-Hand Rule works because it **reduces complexity**. It requires no visual overview, no memory of prior paths, and no understanding of the maze's structure. It succeeds in mazes that are **simply connected**, meaning the exterior and interior are part of one continuous surface. In such mazes, following one wall guarantees traversal of every possible path.

Psychologically, it works because it leverages **motor consistency** over cognitive mapping. It's a default strategy people resort to when they feel lost or overwhelmed.

How It Works

1. Upon entering the maze, place your **left hand** on the wall.

2. Begin walking while maintaining **constant contact** with the wall.

3. At intersections or junctions, continue to follow the wall on your left.

4. Eventually, the path either leads back to the entrance (loop) or to the exit.

This approach is **deterministic**—it avoids getting lost by transforming the maze into a one-dimensional loop.

Application

The Left-Hand Rule is used in:

- **Maze design and solving**: Physical mazes, amusement parks.

- **Robotics**: Simple navigation algorithms for autonomous robots.

- **Search-and-rescue training**: To explore unknown buildings or tunnels.

- **Cognitive science**: As an example of procedural versus strategic problem-solving.

Key Insights

- The Left-Hand Rule highlights how **simple, local rules can solve global problems**.

- It's reliable only in **specific maze types**—it fails in mazes with isolated walls or multiple disconnected sections.

- It reflects how **mechanical heuristics** can outperform complex reasoning under spatial uncertainty.

- The heuristic is easy to execute but lacks **efficiency**—it may lead through every dead end before reaching the goal.

In essence, the Left-Hand Rule demonstrates that **sometimes the best solution isn't clever—it's consistent.**

63. Landmark-based navigation heuristic

Landmark-based navigation is a spatial reasoning heuristic where individuals orient themselves and make navigation decisions based on **recognizable environmental cues**, such as buildings, trees, intersections, statues, or signs. Rather than using abstract representations like maps or coordinates, this heuristic relies on **concrete, memorable features** in the environment to guide movement and recall spatial routes.

This form of navigation is **egocentric and experiential**—decisions are made in relation to the navigator's current position and view. It is deeply embedded in human cognition and is one of the **earliest navigation strategies learned in childhood**, often persisting into adulthood even with access to sophisticated tools like GPS.

Example

Imagine you're navigating a new city. Instead of memorizing a street map, you remember: "Turn left at the bakery, then go straight until the clock tower, then right at the bookstore." These landmarks form **waypoints** in your cognitive map. If a landmark is missing or obscured, you might feel lost—even if you're technically on the correct path.

This heuristic is often used when giving directions: "Go past the gas station, then turn when you see the church," rather than "Go 500 meters, then turn east."

Why It Works

Landmark-based navigation works because **humans are visually and contextually oriented**. Our brains are optimized to recognize patterns, objects, and environmental cues, especially those that are **distinctive, large, or emotionally salient**. Landmarks help reduce the cognitive load required to process spatial data by transforming complex routes into **manageable chunks**.

It's also more **resilient under stress or uncertainty**. In unfamiliar or rapidly changing environments, people tend to revert to this strategy because it's immediate, sensory-based, and doesn't require abstract planning.

How It Works

1. A person moves through an environment, identifying **salient landmarks**.

2. These landmarks are encoded as **anchors** or **decision points**.

3. Navigation decisions are made by recalling and reacting to these reference points.

4. The sequence of landmarks creates a **route memory** that can be replayed when retracing steps or guiding others.

Over time, repeated exposure strengthens the mental map and enhances wayfinding accuracy.

Application

Landmark-based navigation is used in:

- **Driving**: Especially in areas with irregular street layouts.

- **Tourism**: Travelers rely on iconic structures or features.

- **Indoor environments**: Like airports, malls, or hospitals where maps are hard to follow.

- **Robotics and AI**: Some algorithms mimic this strategy using visual SLAM (Simultaneous Localization and Mapping).

- **Cognitive therapy**: Helping individuals with memory impairment navigate familiar environments.

Key Insights

- This heuristic reflects **natural, embodied cognition**— thinking with and through the environment.

- It's fast, intuitive, and **minimizes cognitive effort**, but may fail in sparse or homogeneous settings.

- Individual preferences vary—some people are more **landmark-oriented**, while others prefer **map-based (survey) strategies**.

- It can be **culturally influenced**, as certain societies emphasize spatial directions (north/south) over landmark-based cues.

In essence, landmark-based navigation demonstrates how **humans navigate the world by anchoring movement in meaningful visual cues**, not just geometry.

64. Turn minimizing heuristic

The *Turn Minimizing Heuristic* is a navigation strategy where individuals attempt to reach a destination by selecting paths that require the **fewest number of turns**, especially sharp or complex ones. Rather than optimizing for distance or time, this heuristic simplifies decision-making by reducing the **cognitive and physical effort** involved in navigation. It reflects the principle of minimizing complexity in spatial reasoning—assuming that straighter paths are more direct, less confusing, and easier to remember.

This heuristic is a practical example of bounded rationality: when full optimization is difficult or unnecessary, people opt for **"good enough" solutions** that reduce cognitive demands. It's particularly prevalent in unfamiliar environments or when individuals lack access to maps or digital tools.

Example

Imagine someone walking through a city to find a café. They don't know the exact route but decide to follow streets that require the fewest direction changes—opting to go straight when possible and avoid winding or turning paths. Even if a quicker route exists that involves more turns, the person's path feels more intuitive and easier to manage. This is the turn minimizing heuristic in action.

Similarly, drivers unfamiliar with a city might avoid routes with multiple turns, preferring larger, straighter roads even if the distance is longer. This preference stems from a desire for simplicity and reduced navigational stress.

Why It Works

The turn minimizing heuristic works because it aligns with **cognitive efficiency** and **environmental predictability**. Each turn introduces uncertainty—where to go, how far, and what to expect next. Fewer turns mean fewer opportunities for disorientation, fewer decisions, and fewer chances to make mistakes. Humans naturally gravitate toward **simpler, more predictable patterns**, especially under cognitive load or time constraints.

It also aligns with physical considerations: fewer turns mean fewer stops or slow-downs, which can reduce **travel effort, especially in walking or driving contexts**.

How It Works

1. The individual identifies their current location and goal.

2. When multiple paths are possible, they prioritize routes with **fewer directional changes**.

3. At intersections, preference is given to continuing straight or making minor course corrections rather than major turns.

4. The path taken is typically longer in distance but **simpler in structure**, making it easier to remember and follow.

The heuristic often functions subconsciously, especially in novel or complex environments.

Application

The turn minimizing heuristic is applied in:

- **Urban walking and driving**: Especially when navigating without GPS.

- **Wayfinding system design**: Hospitals, airports, or malls may structure signage to guide users with minimal directional change.

- **Cognitive robotics**: Some AI models replicate this strategy to simplify pathfinding in complex environments.

- **Design of evacuation routes**: Fewer turns lead to quicker, more intuitive escapes.

Key Insights

- The turn minimizing heuristic highlights how **people value simplicity over efficiency** when navigating.

- It reduces **decision fatigue** and error, especially in unfamiliar or high-stakes environments.

- While not always optimal in terms of distance, it's often **superior for usability and confidence**.

- This strategy reflects a broader cognitive principle: **simplify the path to reduce uncertainty**.

In essence, the turn minimizing heuristic illustrates that **in navigation, the easiest route is often the straightest—even if not the shortest**.

65. Euclidean distance heuristic

The *Euclidean Distance Heuristic* is a spatial reasoning strategy used to estimate the **shortest or most direct path between two points** by treating the environment as a flat, continuous space. It assumes that the best route is the one that forms a straight line—based on the geometric principle of **Euclidean distance**, which is the shortest distance between two points in a plane.

This heuristic is widely used in both human navigation and artificial intelligence (particularly in pathfinding algorithms like A*), where an agent must estimate how far a destination is from a given location. It simplifies complex decision-making by substituting an exact path cost with an **approximate "as-the-crow-flies" distance**, often yielding good enough results when speed and simplicity are valued.

Example

Suppose you are in a city and want to reach a park that lies to the northeast of your location. Without knowing the exact layout of the streets, you assume the fastest route is one that heads generally northeast. You navigate using visible landmarks in that direction, perhaps walking diagonally or zig-zagging in a way that follows the park's general line of sight. Even if obstacles like buildings or one-way streets prevent a true straight-line path, your estimation—based on the Euclidean heuristic—guides your general orientation and minimizes perceived detours.

In computer science, an AI agent in a 2D grid world might use the Euclidean distance to estimate the cost to reach a goal node when exploring possible paths, especially when diagonal movement is allowed.

Why It Works

The Euclidean Distance Heuristic works because it provides a **fast and intuitive estimation** of proximity, which is often sufficient in both physical and computational environments. Humans and machines alike benefit from having a **directional bias** toward a goal, especially when the environment is not overly constrained. It reduces the complexity of pathfinding by ignoring intermediate steps or obstacles until they must be considered, supporting efficient planning.

Moreover, our **visual-spatial systems** naturally encode distances and directions in a roughly Euclidean manner, making it cognitively seamless to apply.

How It Works

1. Define the start and end points.

2. Calculate or estimate the **straight-line distance** between them.

3. Use this distance as a heuristic guide for selecting routes or prioritizing options.

4. Adjust as needed when obstacles or constraints arise.

In AI, the Euclidean distance is often used as the heuristic function h(n) in algorithms like A*, where it influences which nodes are explored first.

Application

This heuristic is used in:

- **Human wayfinding**: Navigating cities, parks, or campuses.

- **Pathfinding algorithms**: In robotics, gaming, and GPS systems.

- **Logistics and delivery**: Estimating distances between customer locations.

- **Architecture and UX**: Designing spaces to feel navigable by minimizing perceived distance.

Key Insights

- The Euclidean heuristic is simple but powerful—**fast to compute, easy to use**.

- It works best in **open or grid-like environments** with minimal obstacles.

- It may mislead in complex or constrained environments, where actual travel paths are longer.

- Combining it with other heuristics (e.g., turn cost or terrain penalties) improves accuracy in practical applications.

In essence, the Euclidean Distance Heuristic reveals that **the shortest mental path to a destination is often a straight line— even if the real-world path isn't.**

66. Voronoi heuristic

The *Voronoi Heuristic* is a spatial reasoning strategy grounded in the principles of *Voronoi diagrams*, a concept from computational geometry. A **Voronoi diagram** partitions a space into regions based on proximity to a set of predefined points (called "sites"). Each region contains all points closest to one site than to any other. The Voronoi Heuristic leverages this concept by guiding agents (humans or machines) to move toward the **nearest target, centre, or goal region**, assuming that minimizing distance to the closest site will lead to an optimal or satisfactory outcome.

The heuristic is widely applied in navigation, clustering, territory allocation, and AI pathfinding. It assumes that proximity equates to relevance or efficiency, simplifying decisions when faced with multiple competing destinations.

Example

Imagine a delivery drone that needs to choose which warehouse to fly to for restocking. The city has several evenly distributed warehouses. Instead of analyzing traffic, air corridors, and dynamic demand, the drone uses the Voronoi Heuristic: it identifies which warehouse is closest and heads in that direction. The drone effectively behaves as though the city were divided into Voronoi cells, each assigned to the nearest warehouse.

Though this approach doesn't account for every variable, it often yields fast, "good enough" decisions.

Humans use a similar strategy informally. For instance, when searching for a gas station on a highway, people usually choose the closest one, even if a slightly farther one offers cheaper fuel or better services.

Why It Works

The Voronoi Heuristic works because it **reduces complex spatial problems to simple proximity-based decisions**. The assumption is that in most real-world contexts, **the closest option is also the most efficient**. It's computationally efficient and intuitive, especially in well-distributed environments where options are relatively uniform.

Cognitively, it aligns with how people naturally organize space— by clustering areas around focal points (e.g., nearest school, park, hospital). It supports rapid decision-making without requiring exhaustive evaluation of all options.

How It Works

1. Define all potential goal points or resource sites in a space.

2. Partition the space into **Voronoi cells**—each corresponding to the area nearest to a given site.

3. For any new position (agent, person, object), determine which cell they are in.

4. Select the corresponding site (e.g., service centre, waypoint) as the optimal choice.

This method assumes that **proximity correlates with utility**, and thus the nearest region is the best to pursue.

Application

*   **Pathfinding algorithms**: Used in robotics, video games, and logistics.

*   **Facility location**: Planning services (e.g., schools, fire stations) based on coverage.

*   **Wireless communication**: Assigning users to the closest cell tower.

*   **Crowd simulation**: Modeling movement toward the nearest exit or hub.

*   **Geographic Information Systems (GIS)**: Territory mapping and resource allocation.

Key Insights

*   The Voronoi heuristic provides **quick, spatially rational decisions** with minimal computation.

- It performs best in **uniform or low-obstacle environments** but may mislead where travel cost isn't based purely on distance.

- It's foundational in **decentralized systems**, where agents make independent choices based on local proximity.

- Enhancing it with cost functions or terrain awareness can improve accuracy in complex domains.

In essence, the Voronoi Heuristic captures the principle that **where you are often dictates where you should go next— especially when time is short and options are many**.

67. Waypoint heuristic

The *Waypoint Heuristic* is a spatial navigation strategy in which a person or agent breaks down a complex journey into smaller, manageable segments by identifying and navigating through **intermediate reference points** or "waypoints" en route to a final destination. Instead of plotting a direct path from start to finish, this heuristic simplifies navigation by focusing on a series of local goals. Each waypoint acts as a short-term subgoal that incrementally guides movement toward the ultimate objective.

This approach is highly intuitive and reflects how both humans and machines manage complex environments. By decomposing a path into recognizable checkpoints, the mind or system avoids being overwhelmed by the full complexity of the space. It is used extensively in human cognition, robotics, AI navigation, and video game pathfinding.

Example

Imagine a hiker trying to reach a mountain summit without a detailed map. Rather than attempting to find a direct, optimal route, the hiker might use a **series of visible waypoints**—a large boulder, a stream, a ridge line—as intermediate targets. The hiker reaches one, reorients, and proceeds to the next. Even though the path may not be the shortest, it's **navigable and psychologically manageable**.

Similarly, in GPS-based routing, navigation systems often construct paths that pass through intermediate waypoints like highway exits or notable intersections before arriving at the destination.

Why It Works

The Waypoint Heuristic works because it **reduces cognitive complexity**. Planning an entire route through unfamiliar or dynamic terrain requires sustained mental effort and the processing of large spatial datasets. Waypoints **divide the task into chunks**, allowing for simpler, stepwise planning. This mirrors how working memory functions best with limited, sequential information.

In physical and digital environments alike, waypoints provide a **sense of progress**. Reaching each one acts as positive reinforcement, increasing confidence and reducing perceived distance.

How It Works

1. The overall destination is identified.

2. A set of **intermediate waypoints**—based on visibility, accessibility, or familiarity—are chosen.

3. Navigation proceeds from the current position to the next waypoint.

4. Upon reaching a waypoint, orientation is updated, and the next leg is planned.

5. This continues until the final destination is reached.

Waypoints can be **predefined (e.g., programmed routes)** or **selected dynamically** based on environmental cues.

Application

- **Autonomous robots and drones**: Pathfinding using sequential GPS points.

- **Hiking and orienteering**: Visual navigation via landmarks or checkpoints.

- **Air traffic control**: Aircraft follow fixed waypoints during flights.

- **Video games**: NPCs navigate game environments using path nodes.

- **Urban navigation**: People give and follow directions using turns at known intersections or buildings.

Key Insights

5. The waypoint heuristic reflects **chunking in spatial cognition**, allowing more effective problem-solving over time.

6. It offers **flexibility** and **scalability**—adaptable in both simple and complex environments.

7. While it may not always yield the **shortest path**, it often produces the most **reliable and mentally manageable** one.

8. This approach supports **incremental re-planning**, especially in uncertain or changing conditions.

In essence, the waypoint heuristic shows that **the best way to reach a distant goal is often by focusing on what's directly in front of you—one step at a time**.

68. Manhattan distance heuristic

The *Manhattan Distance Heuristic*—also known as *taxicab geometry* or *city block distance*—is a strategy used in spatial reasoning and pathfinding where movement is restricted to orthogonal (horizontal and vertical) paths. Unlike the Euclidean distance, which measures the direct "as-the-crow-flies" distance, Manhattan distance calculates the **sum of the absolute horizontal and vertical differences** between two points. It's named after the grid-like layout of Manhattan, where vehicles typically move along perpendicular streets.

This heuristic is commonly used in **AI algorithms**, robotics, and maze navigation when the agent can only move in four directions (up, down, left, right). It simplifies complex environments into grid-like frameworks, making path estimation faster and more efficient when diagonal movement isn't allowed.

Example

Imagine you're in a city where streets are laid out in a perfect grid. You're at 1st Avenue and 1st Street, and your destination is at 6th Avenue and 4th Street. Using Manhattan distance, your path must consist of 5 blocks east and 3 blocks north—a total of 8 blocks. Regardless of the actual street layout or obstacles, the **Manhattan distance = |6 - 1| + |4 - 1| = 8**.

This is different from Euclidean distance, which would compute the straight-line distance, resulting in a shorter but often non-navigable route in grid environments.

Why It Works

The Manhattan Distance Heuristic works because it **matches real-world movement constraints** in grid-based systems. Many environments—urban street layouts, circuit boards, game maps—conform to restricted movement directions. In such systems, this heuristic provides a **computationally cheap, accurate approximation** of the shortest path when diagonal movement is not allowed.

Additionally, it simplifies the complexity of pathfinding, reducing the problem to **basic arithmetic**, which allows faster decision-making in both biological and artificial systems.

How It Works

1. Identify the current position (x1, y1) and the goal position (x2, y2).

2. Compute the Manhattan distance:
   Distance = |x2 - x1| + |y2 - y1|

3. Use this value as an **estimate for the cost** to reach the goal.

4. In pathfinding algorithms (e.g., A*), this heuristic helps prioritize nodes that appear closer based on grid-aligned movement.

Because it **underestimates or equals the actual cost** in constrained environments, it remains an **admissible heuristic** in search algorithms.

Application

- **AI pathfinding**: Used in A* for tile-based games or robot movement in 2D grids.

- **Urban navigation**: Estimating pedestrian or vehicle routes in cities with orthogonal street networks.

- **Circuit design**: Routing paths between components on grid-like circuit boards.

- **Warehouse automation**: Robots navigating aisles and shelves using grid-based logic.

Key Insights

- The Manhattan heuristic is ideal where **movement is limited to horizontal and vertical axes**.

- It is **computationally lightweight**, making it efficient in large-scale systems.

- It's most effective in grid-based environments but **inaccurate in systems that allow diagonal or curved movement**.

- The method reflects the broader heuristic principle of **matching estimation strategies to environmental structure**.

In essence, the Manhattan Distance Heuristic teaches that **the best estimate depends on how you're allowed to move—not just where you want to go**.

69. Path following heuristic

The *Path Following Heuristic* is a strategy in navigation and decision-making where an individual or agent chooses to follow a **predefined, visible, or previously travelled path** rather than attempting to calculate or create a new route. This heuristic relies on the assumption that the existing path leads to a desirable or goal-oriented outcome, thereby reducing the mental and computational effort needed to evaluate alternatives. It is often used in both **natural environments (like trails or roads)** and **structured systems (such as digital networks or robotic pathfinding)**.

At its core, this heuristic reflects the principle of **efficiency through repetition**: if a path exists, it likely exists for a reason—because it has been used successfully in the past.

Example

Imagine you're hiking in a forest with several possible routes, but one path is clearly worn from frequent use. Even if it's not marked, you assume it leads somewhere useful—perhaps a viewpoint or an exit. Rather than exploring or attempting a shortcut, you choose to follow the visible trail. That's path following in action: it reduces uncertainty and leverages prior usage as a cue for decision-making.

Similarly, in robotic systems like autonomous vacuums or delivery robots, a path-following heuristic can guide them along

predefined lanes or routes—helping them avoid obstacles or
redundant exploration.

Why It Works

This heuristic works because it **reduces cognitive load and risk**.
When individuals are uncertain, under time pressure, or lacking
complete information, following an existing path offers a **low-
effort, high-trust option**. It leverages the logic of social proof
("others have used this path") and environmental cues (visibility,
wear, or design) to suggest a correct course of action.

Additionally, many paths are created and maintained with
intentionality—roads, hallways, corridors, footpaths—so
adhering to them increases the likelihood of reaching useful
destinations.

How It Works

1. The individual or agent encounters an environment with
   at least one visible or known path.

2. Rather than evaluating every possible direction, they
   choose to **follow the existing path**.

3. Navigation decisions (e.g., turns or stops) are made by
   reacting to the path's structure—curves, intersections,
   and endpoints.

4. Adjustments may occur if the path is blocked, unclear, or
   deviates from the expected goal.

This heuristic is especially useful when **the goal is unknown or only vaguely defined**, but the user assumes the path is a guide toward it.

Application

- **Hiking and trail navigation**: Following worn or marked routes.

- **Warehouse robotics**: Guided paths between shelves and stations.

- **Public building design**: Wayfinding through corridors and signage.

- **Digital systems**: Following hyperlink paths or user flow patterns in UI/UX design.

- **Urban environments**: Pedestrian movement along sidewalks and desire paths.

Key Insights

- The path following heuristic emphasizes **trust in environmental affordances**.

- It is **efficient and reliable**, though not always optimal in distance or speed.

- It reflects the broader human tendency to prefer **predictable and socially validated behaviour**.

- It's particularly powerful in **uncertain or novel situations**, where exploration is risky or costly.

In essence, the path following heuristic teaches that **sometimes, the smartest move is simply to follow the trail already taken**— because paths often encode the wisdom of previous decisions.

70. Dead reckoning heuristic

The *Dead Reckoning Heuristic* is a method of navigation where the current position is estimated based on a known starting point and a record of **direction, speed, and elapsed time**. Rather than relying on external landmarks or signals, dead reckoning projects one's position forward using internal calculations. The heuristic assumes that if the direction and velocity are known and constant, the new position can be estimated by mentally or computationally "walking out" from the last known location.

This method has deep historical roots, originating in nautical navigation long before the invention of GPS or compasses. Today, it is still used in robotics, aviation, and cognitive science to explain how humans and machines estimate location when environmental cues are unavailable or unreliable.

Example

Imagine a hiker walking through dense fog. Without visual landmarks or a GPS, they estimate their position based on the direction they started in (e.g., northeast), how fast they think they're walking (say, 4 km/h), and how long they've been moving (30 minutes). They calculate that they are roughly 2 kilometers northeast of their original position. That's dead reckoning: a self-contained, mental computation of location based on motion data.

Similarly, autonomous underwater vehicles (AUVs) often rely on dead reckoning when GPS signals are unavailable. They integrate speed, heading, and time to estimate their position relative to a launch point.

Why It Works

The dead reckoning heuristic works because it enables **navigation in environments without external feedback**, such as darkness, underwater, or underground. It leverages **internal consistency and motion data**, assuming that errors will be minimal if the environment is relatively stable and movements are deliberate.

Cognitively, humans use similar logic in spatial memory— estimating where something is relative to where they started based on steps taken, turns made, and elapsed time. This heuristic minimizes reliance on memory or environmental mapping.

How It Works

1. Begin with a known position (origin).

2. Track **direction** of movement (via compass, proprioception, or sensors).

3. Measure **speed** or velocity over time.

4. Multiply speed by time in the given direction to calculate the **estimated current position**.

5. Update this position as new movements are made.

Errors accumulate over time, especially if movement isn't constant or direction tracking is imprecise. Therefore, dead reckoning is often paired with periodic corrections using landmarks or GPS (when available).

Application

- **Aviation and maritime navigation**: Estimating positions between radio or GPS signals.

- **Robotics**: Autonomous movement in GPS-denied zones.

- **Cognitive psychology**: Modeling human path integration and spatial awareness.

- **Emergency response**: Navigating smoke-filled or blackout conditions.

- **Gaming and simulations**: AI path estimation in dynamic environments.

Key Insights

- Dead reckoning prioritizes **internal motion data over external feedback**.

- It is efficient and usable when **sensory input is limited**, though prone to drift over time.

- It reflects a fundamental human and animal ability: **path integration**—tracking one's position in space without seeing landmarks.

- Regular recalibration improves accuracy, making it ideal for **hybrid navigation systems**.

In essence, the dead reckoning heuristic shows that even in the absence of guidance, we can **calculate our way forward—step by step—using only where we've been and how we've moved.**

👥 Social and Communication Heuristics

71. Authority heuristic

The *Authority Heuristic* is a cognitive shortcut where individuals defer judgment or decision-making to someone perceived as an authority figure, expert, or leader. Rather than analyzing the facts themselves, people rely on the belief that someone in a position of power or with specialized knowledge is likely to be correct. This heuristic simplifies complex decisions by outsourcing cognitive effort to a perceived trustworthy source.

Rooted in both **social psychology** and **evolutionary reasoning**, the authority heuristic reflects a survival strategy: in uncertain or high-stakes situations, it's often adaptive to follow those who appear more experienced or informed. This tendency is especially powerful in hierarchical environments such as medicine, education, military, or corporate settings.

Example

A classic example is the **Milgram experiment (1960s)**, where participants were instructed by an authority figure (a scientist in a lab coat) to administer what they believed were increasingly painful electric shocks to another person. Despite moral discomfort, most complied, demonstrating the profound influence of perceived authority.

In everyday life, individuals might take a medication because a doctor prescribed it, invest in a product because a celebrity endorsed it, or accept a legal opinion because a judge or lawyer gave it—even if they don't fully understand the underlying reasons.

Why It Works

The authority heuristic works because it **reduces cognitive burden and decision-making time**. Evaluating complex information (medical, technical, legal, etc.) requires expertise and effort. By trusting someone perceived as more knowledgeable, individuals can act with greater speed and confidence, especially in high-uncertainty situations.

Moreover, from a social cohesion perspective, societies function more efficiently when individuals **respect expertise and established roles**. Historically, following experienced leaders could increase group survival in emergencies or unfamiliar environments.

How It Works

1. A decision or judgment is required in an uncertain or unfamiliar domain.

2. An authority figure is recognized—through **titles, symbols (e.g., uniforms), credentials**, or reputation.

3. The individual **defers to the authority's judgment** rather than analyzing independently.

4. The decision is made based on the **credibility of the source**, not just the content.

This process can be either conscious ("I trust the expert") or subconscious ("They look official").

Application

- **Medicine**: Patients complying with doctors' instructions without understanding the diagnosis.

- **Marketing**: Endorsements from experts or influencers to drive product credibility.

- **Legal systems**: Jurors influenced by testimony from recognized professionals.

- **Education**: Students accepting information as true based on teacher expertise.

- **Public policy**: Citizens following rules based on statements from government officials.

Key Insights

- The authority heuristic can **save time and promote social order**, but it also introduces risk if the authority is unqualified or unethical.

- Symbols of authority (titles, clothing, certifications) **amplify compliance**, even when actual expertise is absent.

- Critical thinking can be diminished when **authority overrides evidence**.

- Awareness of this heuristic is essential in contexts where **manipulation or misinformation** is possible.

In essence, the authority heuristic shows that in moments of uncertainty, we often **trust the voice that sounds the most certain—whether or not it should be.**

72. Reciprocity heuristic

The *Reciprocity Heuristic* is a social decision-making shortcut based on the expectation that **favors or benefits received should be returned in kind**. It operates on the simple principle: *"If someone does something for me, I should do something for them."* This heuristic is deeply rooted in human evolutionary psychology and is a foundational rule in virtually all cultures. It plays a crucial role in maintaining social cooperation, trust, and fairness by encouraging mutual exchange and discouraging freeloading.

Rather than carefully weighing the costs and benefits of returning a favour, individuals often respond automatically— driven by a social norm that promotes **balanced give-and-take**. The reciprocity heuristic reduces the complexity of social interactions and reinforces cohesion within groups by motivating cooperation and reducing conflict.

Example

A classic example can be seen in marketing. If a salesperson offers a free sample—say, a piece of chocolate in a shop— customers are significantly more likely to make a purchase. The gift, however small, triggers an internal urge to reciprocate the gesture, often with a purchase or positive behaviour in return.

Similarly, in social relationships, if a colleague helps you with a task, you're more inclined to return the favour—even if it's inconvenient—because of the built-in pressure to uphold the balance of kindness.

Why It Works

The reciprocity heuristic works because it **reinforces prosocial behaviour**. In early human societies, where survival depended on cooperation, those who reciprocated were more likely to form alliances and be supported by others. Over time, this evolved into a near-universal social expectation: **failures to reciprocate often result in social disapproval or exclusion**.

From a cognitive standpoint, the heuristic allows for **rapid social decisions**. Rather than calculating whether returning a favour is rational or beneficial, people rely on a built-in rule: return what was given, even if the exchange is unequal in value.

How It Works

1. An individual receives a gift, favour, or service.

2. This creates an **internal or social obligation** to respond in kind.

3. When an opportunity arises, the individual **reciprocates**, even if no explicit request was made.

4. The behaviour reinforces the social bond and encourages future cooperation.

This process may occur consciously (out of gratitude) or subconsciously (to avoid guilt or maintain reputation).

Application

- **Marketing and sales**: Free trials, samples, or gifts encourage customer reciprocation through purchases or loyalty.

- **Negotiations**: Making a concession encourages the other party to match it.

- **Workplace dynamics**: Favors exchanged informally can foster collaboration.

- **International diplomacy**: Aid or support is often reciprocated through alliances or policy support.

- **Charity appeals**: Sending small gifts in donation mailers increases contributions.

Key Insights

- The reciprocity heuristic is a powerful **social glue**, but also a **vulnerability** when exploited manipulatively.

- It drives **compliance, generosity, and trust**, even when logic suggests restraint.

- The **value of the initial gift** doesn't have to match the return—the act itself triggers the urge to reciprocate.

- Recognizing this heuristic enables both more ethical influence and better resistance to undue pressure.

In essence, the reciprocity heuristic reflects the enduring human truth: **we're wired to return kindness, often more than we realize.**

73. Liking heuristic

The *Liking Heuristic* is a social cognitive shortcut where individuals are more likely to agree with, follow, or be persuaded by people they **like**. Rather than evaluating the message, offer, or argument on its own merit, people rely on their **affective response** to the source. If the communicator is friendly, attractive, similar, or warm, the message is more readily accepted. This heuristic reflects how **emotional rapport often overrides rational analysis** in decision-making.

The concept has been explored extensively in social psychology, notably by Robert Cialdini in his work on influence. The heuristic operates in personal interactions, advertising, politics, and negotiation—where **likability becomes a powerful form of persuasion**.

Example

Imagine you're approached by two salespeople offering the same product. One is distant and robotic, the other is friendly, shares your interests, and makes you feel comfortable. Even though the product is identical, you're far more likely to buy from the second salesperson. That's the liking heuristic at work—**positive emotional cues influence your trust and willingness to comply**.

In another context, consider celebrity endorsements. People are often swayed to purchase products endorsed by actors, athletes, or influencers they like—even if those individuals have no expertise related to the product. The emotional connection to the celebrity drives the decision more than rational evaluation.

Why It Works

The liking heuristic works because humans are **social creatures** attuned to cues of safety, warmth, and affiliation. Evolutionarily, trusting and aligning with those we like helped form stable groups, which increased chances of survival. Psychologically, we assume that likable people have **positive intent**, are more trustworthy, and are likely to make fair offers.

Moreover, liking often leads to **reduced skepticism**. When we like someone, we tend to give them the benefit of the doubt, making us more susceptible to persuasion and influence.

How It Works

1. A person forms a **positive emotional impression** of someone—based on friendliness, appearance, shared values, compliments, or humor.

2. This emotional judgment **biases cognitive evaluations**, making us more receptive to suggestions or arguments from that person.

3. As a result, we comply, agree, or follow through—**not necessarily because the idea is strong**, but because the source feels trustworthy and appealing.

Application

- **Sales and marketing**: Friendly and charismatic representatives increase conversion rates.

- **Advertising**: Likable spokespersons or characters (e.g., Flo from Progressive) create brand loyalty.

- **Politics**: Candidates emphasize relatability and charm to sway voters.

- **Negotiation**: Building rapport can increase concession and cooperation.

- **Workplace leadership**: Managers who are liked tend to receive more cooperation, even in tough situations.

Key Insights

- The liking heuristic **bypasses logical scrutiny**, relying on emotional shortcuts.

- Likability can be **engineered**—through flattery, similarity, or familiarity—which can make people vulnerable to manipulation.

- This heuristic shows that **who delivers the message** often matters more than the message itself.

- Being aware of this tendency can **improve resistance to undue influence** and foster more objective decision-making.

In essence, the liking heuristic illustrates a powerful truth: **we're more likely to say "yes" to those we like—even when we shouldn't.**

74. In-group bias heuristic

The *In-Group Bias Heuristic* is a social-cognitive shortcut in which individuals automatically favour members of their own group—defined by shared identity, values, background, or affiliation—over those in an out-group. This favouritism often emerges unconsciously and influences **judgments, trust, cooperation, and resource allocation**. Rather than evaluating people or ideas on merit alone, individuals rely on group membership as a **proxy for reliability, morality, or competence**.

Rooted in **social identity theory** (Tajfel & Turner, 1979), this heuristic reflects how humans are evolutionarily wired to categorize others into "us" vs. "them." This distinction helped early humans navigate alliances, threats, and resource competition, and it continues to shape behaviour in modern social, political, and organizational settings.

Example

Consider a workplace scenario in which an employee must choose between two equally qualified candidates for a project: one is a close colleague from the same team (in-group), and the other is from a different department (out-group). Despite equal capabilities, the employee selects their teammate, justifying the decision based on "better chemistry" or "past collaboration"—even though those may not be objective criteria.

Another example occurs in sports fandom. Supporters of a particular team often view referees as biased when a call goes against their team, while excusing the same calls when made in their favour. This selective perception is a manifestation of in-group bias.

Why It Works

In-group bias works because it **reduces social uncertainty** and **enhances group cohesion**. By trusting those who are similar or familiar, individuals can coordinate more easily, avoid conflict, and increase their own sense of safety and belonging. It also boosts **self-esteem**, as identifying with a high-status or successful in-group enhances one's perceived value.

From a cognitive standpoint, categorizing people into groups helps simplify complex social environments—allowing for faster, albeit sometimes biased, judgments.

How It Works

1. The mind categorizes individuals into in-group (us) and out-group (them), often based on visible cues, labels, or shared experiences.

2. Positive attributes (trustworthiness, intelligence, loyalty) are **more readily assigned to in-group members**.

3. Decisions, support, and empathy are **disproportionately directed toward the in-group**, often at the expense of fairness or objectivity.

This process is largely automatic, though it can be moderated through awareness and deliberate effort.

Application

- **Hiring and promotion**: Favoritism toward people with shared backgrounds.

- **Politics**: Voter loyalty based on party identity, not policy.

- **Education**: Teachers unknowingly favoring students from similar socio-cultural groups.

- **Conflict resolution**: Difficulty empathizing with opposing sides.

- **Marketing**: Brands positioning themselves as part of a consumer's "tribe" (e.g., Apple users vs. Android users).

Key Insights

- In-group bias enhances **social bonding but impairs objectivity**.

- It operates at both **conscious and unconscious levels**, often without malicious intent.

- It can fuel **prejudice, discrimination, and polarization** when left unchecked.

- Encouraging **cross-group collaboration and shared identities** (e.g., "we're all part of the same mission") can reduce its impact.

In essence, the in-group bias heuristic reflects the powerful pull of "us"—but reminds us that fairness begins when we question who "us" really includes.

75. Tit-for-tat heuristic

The *Tit-for-Tat Heuristic* is a simple, yet powerful strategy used in social decision-making, cooperation, and game theory. At its core, the heuristic follows a straightforward rule: **start cooperatively, then mirror your counterpart's previous behaviour**. If the other party cooperates, you continue cooperating. If they defect or act selfishly, you retaliate by doing the same. This reciprocal strategy is grounded in both **evolutionary theory** and **strategic interaction models**, especially within the context of repeated or iterated games like the *Prisoner's Dilemma*.

Tit-for-tat exemplifies a **bounded rationality** heuristic—it simplifies decision-making in complex social environments by using a short memory (just the previous round's behaviour) rather than requiring exhaustive calculations or predictive modelling. It has been shown to be robust, adaptive, and surprisingly effective in promoting **long-term cooperation** among self-interested individuals.

Example

Consider two businesses negotiating a long-term partnership. Initially, one company offers favourable contract terms. The second company reciprocates with transparency and timely deliveries. However, if one party starts exploiting loopholes or delaying payments, the other may respond in kind by tightening contract clauses or delaying their own obligations. This pattern of mutual cooperation or retaliation is a real-world enactment of the tit-for-tat heuristic: respond in kind to maintain balance and signal expectations.

In classic experiments of the iterated Prisoner's Dilemma, players using tit-for-tat consistently outperformed more complex or aggressive strategies, especially in environments where repeated interaction encouraged mutual monitoring.

Why It Works

Tit-for-tat works because it strikes an effective balance between **generosity and protection**. It begins with cooperation (promoting goodwill) but quickly punishes betrayal (discouraging exploitation). This balance ensures it is **not easily exploited**, while remaining **forgiving**—allowing relationships to reset and recover after conflict.

It leverages core human psychological tendencies toward **reciprocity**, **fairness**, and **social learning**. Individuals recognize patterns and adjust their behaviour based on others' responses, making tit-for-tat a clear and easily understood rule of engagement.

How It Works

1. Begin with cooperation (a generous move).

2. In subsequent rounds, observe the counterpart's behaviour.

3. **Repeat their last action**—cooperate if they cooperated, retaliate if they defected.

4. Maintain the cycle, adapting only if their behaviour changes.

This minimalistic strategy requires **little cognitive effort** and works effectively in both interpersonal and institutional settings.

Application

- **Negotiation and diplomacy**: Encouraging fair trade and penalizing unfair actions.

- **Online communities**: Users reciprocating helpfulness or reporting bad behaviour.

- **Parenting and education**: Reinforcing positive behaviour while discouraging misconduct through consistent mirroring.

- **Business relationships**: Rewarding loyalty or penalizing breaches in trust.

- **Evolutionary biology**: Explains altruism and punishment behaviours among social animals.

Key Insights

- Tit-for-tat promotes **sustainable cooperation** in environments with ongoing interaction.

- It is **easy to understand, implement, and predict**, enhancing transparency and trust.

- The strategy's strength lies in its **clarity and consistency—** both cooperative and retaliatory.

- While highly effective, it can struggle in noisy environments where actions are misinterpreted; adding forgiveness (e.g., "Tit-for-two-tats") can improve resilience.

In essence, the tit-for-tat heuristic shows that **fairness doesn't require complexity—just consistency, memory, and mutual respect**.

76. Reputation-based heuristic

The *Reputation-Based Heuristic* is a decision-making shortcut in which individuals base their trust, cooperation, or selection of others on **perceived reputation** rather than direct experience or detailed information. It allows people to make relatively safe and fast judgments in uncertain social environments by leveraging **social feedback**, shared opinions, or prior behaviours associated with a person, group, or organization.

Rooted in **evolutionary psychology** and **game theory**, this heuristic functions as a survival strategy—helping individuals avoid harm and align with trustworthy others. In modern settings, it's widely used in both offline interactions (e.g., choosing a mechanic recommended by neighbours) and online environments (e.g., using user reviews to pick products).

Example

Imagine you're looking for a freelance designer for a project. You don't know anyone personally, so you turn to a platform like Upwork or Fiverr. There, you scan reviews and ratings. One designer has five stars and glowing testimonials from dozens of clients; another has no reviews at all. Even though you've never met the first designer, you're far more likely to hire them. That's the reputation-based heuristic in action: **prior positive evaluations serve as a proxy for trustworthiness**.

In evolutionary terms, early humans likely relied on reputational signals—stories, gossip, or observed behaviour—to decide who to cooperate with or avoid in the group.

Why It Works

This heuristic works because **direct observation or verification isn't always possible**. Time, resources, or access may be limited, so relying on the social judgments of others helps reduce risk. Reputations aggregate **multiple data points into a single, simplified cue**—such as "reliable," "dishonest," or "fair"— allowing for faster decisions.

Furthermore, maintaining a good reputation incentivizes prosocial behaviour. Individuals or organizations that know they're being watched or rated are more likely to act fairly, making reputation not only informative but also regulatory.

How It Works

1. A person lacks full information about another's capabilities, intentions, or past actions.

2. They look for **reputational cues**: reviews, word of mouth, ratings, or public behaviour.

3. These cues inform their decision to **trust, cooperate, avoid, or invest**.

4. Reputation may be updated over time as new information or experiences are gathered.

This heuristic often overlaps with **social proof** but is more specifically tied to **historical accountability** rather than popularity alone.

Application

- **E-commerce**: Star ratings and customer reviews guide consumer choices.

- **Gig economy**: Platforms like Airbnb, Uber, and TaskRabbit rely heavily on user reputation.

- **Academic and professional fields**: Hiring decisions often consider reputational prestige of prior institutions or mentors.

- **Online communities**: Moderation, trustworthiness, and collaboration are often governed by user history.

- **Political or public trust**: Voters evaluate politicians based on past behaviour and perceived consistency.

Key Insights

- Reputation-based heuristics help manage **uncertainty and risk** in social decision-making.

- They promote accountability—**people behave better when their reputation matters**.

- The heuristic can be manipulated (e.g., fake reviews), so **critical evaluation of reputational sources** is important.

- It highlights how **indirect knowledge can be as influential as personal experience**.

In essence, the reputation-based heuristic reveals how **what others say about you often shapes how others treat you—even before they meet you.**

77. Norm-following heuristic

The *Norm-Following Heuristic* is a social decision-making strategy where individuals guide their behaviour based on what is perceived as typical, expected, or acceptable within a given group or context. Instead of calculating the most rational or optimal course of action, individuals default to **social norms—** implicit or explicit rules that govern behaviour. This heuristic enables people to **act efficiently and socially appropriately**, especially in unfamiliar or ambiguous situations.

This heuristic is deeply embedded in **cultural evolution** and social psychology, reflecting how groups maintain order, identity, and cohesion. From early human tribes to modern societies, conforming to norms has served as a proxy for trustworthiness and group alignment, reducing the need for explicit rules or enforcement.

Example

Imagine you're dining at a formal restaurant for the first time. You're unsure about the etiquette—how to use the utensils, when to order, how to interact with the server. Instead of overthinking each step, you **observe what others are doing** and mimic their behaviour. You follow the dress code, wait to eat until everyone is served, and leave a tip because everyone else does. This is the norm-following heuristic in action—relying on group behaviour as a guide to what's "right."

On a broader scale, drivers who adopt the local custom of yielding at informal intersections—even if laws differ—are using this heuristic to blend into social traffic expectations.

Why It Works

The norm-following heuristic works because it **reduces uncertainty and cognitive load**. Instead of evaluating every choice on its own merits, norms provide **ready-made behavioural scripts**. This is particularly valuable in socially sensitive contexts where incorrect behaviour can lead to embarrassment, conflict, or exclusion.

Norms also signal **in-group belonging**. People who follow norms are seen as more trustworthy, cooperative, and aligned with the group's values—strengthening social bonds and improving coordination.

How It Works

1. An individual encounters a social or situational context.

2. They **observe or recall the prevailing norms**—what others are doing or what is culturally expected.

3. The individual adjusts their behaviour to align with these expectations, often **without explicit deliberation**.

4. Conformity reinforces the norm, encouraging others to follow it too.

This creates a self-reinforcing cycle where **norms guide behaviour and behaviour strengthens norms**.

Application

- **Organizational culture**: Employees adapt to dress codes, meeting behaviour, and communication styles.

- **Public health**: Mask-wearing or hand-washing during pandemics spreads through visible norm adherence.

- **Consumer behaviour**: People buy eco-friendly products when they believe their peers do too.

- **Digital spaces**: Online community rules shape posting and interaction behaviour.

- **Legal compliance**: People follow rules more consistently when they perceive that "most people do."

Key Insights

- Norm-following facilitates **social harmony** but may also discourage innovation or moral dissent.

- It can lead to **both prosocial and harmful behaviours**, depending on the nature of the norm.

- People are especially likely to follow norms when they are **uncertain, new to a group, or under observation**.

- Changing norms (e.g., around inclusivity or sustainability) often begins with **visible norm-breakers** who trigger new defaults.

In essence, the norm-following heuristic highlights that **we often do what others do—not because it's best, but because it feels expected and safe.**

78. Heuristic trust model

The *Heuristic Trust Model* is a mental shortcut used to assess whether or not to trust another individual, system, or entity in a given context—**without engaging in exhaustive analysis**. Instead of evaluating all possible evidence or risks, the decision to trust is based on a few salient cues, such as **familiarity, reputation, appearance, similarity, or authority**. This model enables **fast and efficient judgments**, especially under uncertainty or time constraints.

Trust is a critical component of human interaction, from personal relationships to digital security. However, trust decisions are often made with **limited or incomplete information**, making heuristics an essential part of the process. The heuristic trust model doesn't aim for perfect accuracy—it trades depth for **speed and functional adequacy** in everyday environments.

Example

Consider someone choosing an online vendor. One site is sleek, uses familiar branding, and features verified badges and positive reviews. Another has no reviews, inconsistent design, and unclear policies. Most people will instinctively trust the first site, even without checking every detail. The trust decision hinges on **heuristic cues**—not comprehensive analysis. These cues act as cognitive shortcuts to assess trustworthiness, especially in unfamiliar contexts like digital marketplaces.

In interpersonal scenarios, people may trust someone who makes eye contact, speaks confidently, or shares similar interests—even if they lack deeper knowledge about that person's history or intentions.

Why It Works

The heuristic trust model works because it helps people **navigate social complexity and risk** with limited cognitive resources. Evaluating every detail about someone's trustworthiness is often impractical or impossible, especially in fast-moving or high-pressure situations. Relying on a few **reliable cues** offers an efficient way to make decisions that are "good enough" most of the time.

Evolutionarily, early humans had to make quick decisions about whom to trust for cooperation, protection, or sharing resources—making trust heuristics an adaptive shortcut.

How It Works

1. A situation arises where trust is required (e.g., choosing a partner, using a website, delegating a task).

2. The brain looks for **simple cues or signals** associated with trustworthiness—such as tone, appearance, social validation, or prior interaction.

3. If enough positive cues are detected, the person **grants trust**, even in the absence of complete information.

4. Trust may be updated or revoked over time, but the initial decision is **heuristically driven**.

Application

- **Online platforms**: Trust signals like "verified user" badges, reviews, or SSL icons.

- **Workplace dynamics**: Quick judgments about colleague reliability based on demeanor or group membership.

- **AI and automation**: Users trusting autonomous systems based on design cues (e.g., voice assistants sounding human).

- **Healthcare**: Patients trusting doctors who exhibit warmth and confidence.

- **Cybersecurity**: Users choosing apps or websites that appear professional and familiar.

Key Insights

- Heuristic trust decisions are **fast, intuitive, and often subconscious**.

- These shortcuts work well in many cases but are vulnerable to **manipulation** (e.g., fake reviews or deceptive appearances).

- Trust is situational—people may **trust different cues in different contexts** (e.g., online vs. face-to-face).

- Awareness of the heuristic model helps users balance **efficiency with critical thinking**, especially in high-stakes decisions.

In essence, the heuristic trust model shows that **we often trust based not on proof—but on patterns, signals, and social intuition.**

79. Empathy heuristic

The *Empathy Heuristic* is a cognitive shortcut in which individuals make decisions, judgments, or take actions based on their **emotional identification with others' feelings or experiences**. Rather than engaging in rational analysis or long-term cost–benefit evaluations, this heuristic relies on an **empathic response**—"I feel what they feel"—to guide behaviour. It serves as a **fast, affect-driven mechanism** for fostering prosocial behaviour, cooperation, and moral decision-making.

Empathy, in this context, refers not just to understanding another person's emotional state (cognitive empathy), but to **experiencing a form of emotional resonance** (affective empathy) that prompts quick, often automatic, decisions aimed at helping or aligning with others.

Example

A well-known demonstration of the empathy heuristic occurs in charitable giving. For instance, when people are shown a picture and personal story of a single suffering child (e.g., "Rokia, a 7-year-old from Mali"), they are more likely to donate than when shown statistics about thousands in need. The individual story elicits empathy, which shortcuts more abstract reasoning about impact or efficiency. The decision to help is based on **emotional immediacy** rather than analytical evaluation.

Why It Works

The empathy heuristic works because it activates **deeply rooted social and evolutionary mechanisms**. As social animals, humans have evolved to respond quickly to others' emotional cues— especially distress, joy, and pain—because doing so historically promoted group cohesion, caregiving, and mutual survival.

Empathic feelings **focus attention and mobilize action**, bypassing the slower, more deliberative systems involved in reasoning. It helps people act **morally and cooperatively**, particularly when time or information is limited. This mechanism also reduces psychological distance, making others' needs feel immediate and personally relevant.

How It Works

1. A person observes or hears about another's emotional state (e.g., suffering, joy, anxiety).

2. This triggers an **affective response**—the observer feels a version of that emotion.

3. The emotional reaction acts as a **heuristic cue** for decision-making—such as helping, comforting, or changing behaviour.

4. The individual then takes action (or refrains from harmful action), often without extensive deliberation.

This process is fast, intuitive, and **heavily context-dependent**, often shaped by proximity, similarity, or vividness of the target.

Application

- **Healthcare**: Clinicians using empathetic listening to guide patient care.

- **Education**: Teachers adjusting their responses based on students' visible frustration or enthusiasm.

- **Charity campaigns**: Personalized storytelling to increase donations and engagement.

- **Conflict resolution**: Mediators prompting parties to understand each other's emotions to de-escalate tension.

- **User experience (UX) design**: Empathy mapping to align digital experiences with user needs and frustrations.

Key Insights

- The empathy heuristic promotes **compassionate and socially adaptive behaviour**.

- It can be **biased toward individuals over groups**, and more easily triggered by those perceived as similar or "deserving."

- While effective for fast, prosocial action, it may lead to **inequitable resource allocation** if over-relied upon.

- Empathy-driven decisions are often **more emotionally satisfying**, even when not the most "rational" choice.

In essence, the empathy heuristic demonstrates that **feeling for others is not just moral—it's also a fast, efficient way to decide how to act.**

80. Imitation heuristic

The *Imitation Heuristic* is a cognitive shortcut in which individuals make decisions or adopt behaviours by observing and copying others, especially those perceived as successful, knowledgeable, or socially accepted. Rather than analyzing all options or outcomes independently, people rely on **behavioural cues from others as a proxy for optimal action**. This heuristic plays a crucial role in social learning, cultural transmission, and adaptation in uncertain or complex environments.

The imitation heuristic is rooted in **evolutionary psychology and developmental science**. For early humans, copying others—especially elders or group leaders—helped ensure survival by efficiently transmitting skills, norms, and knowledge without trial-and-error learning. Today, imitation continues to be a fast, efficient method of decision-making, especially when **time, information, or expertise is limited**.

Example

Consider someone who is new to a gym and unfamiliar with how to use the machines. Instead of reading all the instructions or asking for guidance, they watch others using the equipment and mimic what they see. Similarly, in unfamiliar social settings (like formal dinners, religious services, or business meetings), people often **observe and mirror the behaviour of others** to avoid making social missteps.

In marketing, consumers may imitate purchasing behaviour by following trends or influencers—not because they've researched the product in depth, but because they assume that if others are doing it, it's probably right.

Why It Works

The imitation heuristic works because it **reduces cognitive load** and speeds up decision-making in complex or unfamiliar environments. By copying others—especially those seen as competent or successful—individuals can bypass the risks of making mistakes or investing time in exhaustive evaluation.

From an evolutionary standpoint, imitation enabled rapid cultural learning and **adaptive behaviour** within social groups. It's also a way to **build social cohesion**, as mimicking others can signal affiliation and shared norms.

How It Works

1. An individual faces uncertainty about how to behave, choose, or act.

2. They observe the behaviour of others—especially **high-status, expert, or in-group members**.

3. They copy that behaviour, assuming it is **effective or socially acceptable**.

4. The behaviour is reinforced through **positive outcomes or social approval**.

This process is often unconscious and automatic, though it can be deliberate when someone explicitly seeks a role model or expert to emulate.

Application

- **Consumer behaviour**: People buying products endorsed by peers, celebrities, or influencers.

- **Child development**: Children learning language, manners, and skills through imitation.

- **Workplace culture**: New employees adopt norms by copying seasoned colleagues.

- **Education**: Students mirror teacher behaviours or peer study habits.

- **Digital platforms**: Viral trends spread as users imitate what's popular or "liked."

Key Insights

- Imitation is **adaptive** but can also propagate errors or fads.

- The heuristic is strongest under **uncertainty, time pressure, or low expertise**.

- It favors **conformity over innovation**, which can either stabilize or stifle progress.

- Identifying **who gets imitated** (experts, peers, influencers) shapes how behaviours and ideas spread.

- Being aware of this heuristic can help individuals choose **better role models** and resist uncritical conformity.

In essence, the imitation heuristic shows that **we often learn what to do by watching others—even when we don't fully understand why.**

💼 **Practical/Problem-Solving Heuristics**

81. Means-ends analysis heuristic

Means-Ends Analysis (MEA) is a problem-solving heuristic that involves breaking down a goal into subgoals and then identifying the actions (means) necessary to reduce the difference between the current state and the desired end state. Rather than solving the problem in one giant leap, this heuristic systematically narrows the gap between "where you are" and "where you want to be" through a **step-by-step approach**. It is foundational in cognitive psychology and artificial intelligence, particularly in modelling how humans and machines solve complex problems.

The theory was introduced by Newell and Simon (1972) in the context of **problem-solving research**, where they observed that people don't blindly search through all possible actions. Instead, they intelligently reduce the problem space by constantly comparing the current state to the goal and taking directed steps to reduce the difference.

Example

Suppose you're planning a trip to a remote village in another country. You can't just "go there" immediately. You might begin by identifying major subgoals: book a flight to the country, arrange ground transportation to a nearby city, and then secure local transport to the village. Each subgoal gets you closer to the final destination. Whenever an obstacle arises (e.g., no direct flight), you find a means to overcome it (e.g., connect via another city), continuing the cycle of reducing the discrepancy between your current position and your goal.

This reflects the classic MEA pattern: recognize a difference, reduce it with an action, reassess, and repeat.

Why It Works

The heuristic works because it **breaks complex problems into manageable parts**, allowing for incremental progress. Human cognitive resources are limited; MEA provides a structured method that avoids overwhelm by narrowing attention to **one actionable difference at a time**. This reduces decision fatigue and provides continuous feedback, reinforcing problem-solving momentum.

Additionally, MEA incorporates **feedback loops**—each step updates the current state and refines the plan, making the process dynamic and adaptive.

How It Works

1. **Identify the current state** and the desired goal state.

2. **Compare the two** to find the largest or most relevant difference.

3. **Select an operation** (means) that reduces that difference.

4. **Apply the operation** and assess the new state.

5. **Repeat the process** until the goal is reached or no further progress is possible.

This step-by-step loop allows for **focused problem-solving** without exhaustive search.

Application

- **AI and robotics**: Used in automated planning systems and decision trees.

- **Education**: Students solving math or logic problems often intuitively use MEA by tackling smaller parts.

- **Software design**: Programmers use MEA to iteratively debug or optimize code.

- **Business strategy**: Project planning often involves breaking long-term goals into intermediate deliverables.

Key Insights

- MEA is most effective when goals and current states can be clearly defined and **differences are measurable**.

- It helps in **structuring unstructured problems**, especially when full solutions aren't immediately obvious.

- The heuristic promotes **goal-oriented thinking**, focusing effort on actions that move the process forward.

- It can sometimes **stall** when no clear operation reduces the difference, requiring creativity or temporary backtracking.

In essence, means-ends analysis shows that **solving big problems is often a matter of reducing small gaps, one step at a time.**

82. Trial and error heuristic

Trial and Error is a fundamental problem-solving heuristic where individuals attempt multiple solutions or actions until the correct or desired outcome is achieved. Rather than relying on deep theoretical analysis or abstract planning, this heuristic involves **iterative experimentation**, learning through feedback from each attempt. If an action doesn't work, another is tried, and the process continues until success is found or the problem is abandoned.

This approach is considered one of the **earliest and most universal** forms of learning, observable in both humans and animals. The concept has been extensively studied in behavioural psychology, particularly in the work of **Edward Thorndike**, whose puzzle box experiments with cats demonstrated how learning could occur through repeated attempts and elimination of unsuccessful behaviours.

Example

Consider a child trying to open a combination lock without knowing the code. They begin by randomly turning the dial and testing combinations. After several failed attempts, they might notice that a specific number clicks more smoothly into place, prompting them to adjust their strategy. Eventually, they discover the correct sequence. Although inefficient at first, each error provides feedback, guiding future trials.

In everyday life, people often rely on trial and error when assembling flat-pack furniture without reading the instructions— trying one piece, seeing if it fits, and making adjustments based on the result.

Why It Works

The trial and error heuristic works because it **enables learning in uncertain or unfamiliar situations**, especially when no clear rules or instructions exist. It's particularly valuable when the solution space is large or when theoretical reasoning is infeasible.

From an evolutionary perspective, this approach allowed early humans and animals to adapt quickly to new environments by **testing actions and retaining what works**. Errors become informative: they rule out ineffective paths, bringing the problem-solver incrementally closer to the solution.

Additionally, trial and error supports **exploration**, which can lead to innovative or unexpected outcomes that more structured methods might overlook.

How It Works

1. The individual identifies a goal or problem but lacks a clear path to a solution.

2. They attempt a **first possible action** or strategy.

3. Based on feedback (success or failure), they either repeat, modify, or discard the attempt.

4. Over time, **effective behaviours are reinforced**, and ineffective ones are abandoned.

5. Eventually, a working solution is found, often becoming part of long-term learning.

Application

- **Scientific discovery**: Many breakthroughs, like penicillin or vulcanized rubber, resulted from trial and error.

- **Programming**: Debugging code often involves tweaking parts until errors disappear.

- **Medicine**: Diagnosing complex conditions can involve iterative testing and symptom management.

- **Everyday tasks**: Cooking without a recipe, learning new software, or fixing broken appliances.

- **Education**: Students often learn math or puzzles through repeated attempts.

Key Insights

- Trial and error is **accessible, intuitive, and universally applicable**.

- It emphasizes **learning by doing**, which can foster deeper understanding than passive observation.

- It is best suited to **low-risk, high-feedback environments**.

- While powerful, it can be **inefficient or costly** if used without boundaries or reflection.

- Encouraging a safe space to fail enhances its effectiveness, especially in learning contexts.

In essence, trial and error reminds us that **failure is not the opposite of success—but often the path to it.**

83. Working backwards heuristic

Working Backwards is a problem-solving heuristic that involves starting from the desired goal state and reasoning in reverse to determine the steps needed to reach that goal from the current state. Rather than moving linearly forward from the starting point, this heuristic inverts the typical approach, making it especially useful in situations where the end is clear, but the path to get there is not.

This method is rooted in cognitive science and is often applied in **mathematics, logic puzzles, planning, and strategic thinking**. It helps narrow the problem space by anchoring thought on the final objective, allowing the solver to **eliminate irrelevant paths** and focus on steps that directly contribute to reaching the goal.

Example

A classic example is the *Water Jug Problem*, where you must measure out a specific amount of water using only two jugs of fixed capacities. Instead of pouring water in random sequences, one might ask, "What would the final step look like?"—for example, having exactly 4 liters in one jug. The solver can then reason backwards: "What steps could directly produce that state?"—and so on, until arriving at the starting condition.

In real life, consider planning a surprise party. If the goal is for the guest of honor to arrive at 7:00 PM and be surprised, you work backwards: guests need to arrive by 6:30 PM, the food must be ready by 6:00 PM, decorations up by 5:00 PM, and so on. This reverse planning ensures everything aligns with the desired outcome.

Why It Works

Working backwards is effective because it transforms an ill-defined or complex problem into a **clear sequence of manageable sub-steps**. Starting from the end provides clarity and direction, often revealing **dependencies** or **constraints** that might be missed when working forwards. It also helps avoid wasted effort by focusing only on actions that logically contribute to the goal.

This heuristic capitalizes on **goal anchoring**—keeping attention fixed on the final objective—which reduces cognitive load and enhances problem structure.

How It Works

1. **Identify the goal state** clearly and concretely.

2. Ask, "What must immediately precede this goal?" or "What conditions are required for this to occur?"

3. Continue tracing backwards in **reverse steps**, gradually building a path from the goal to the start.

4. Once the path is complete, **reverse the sequence** to produce the action plan moving forward.

This approach is often visualized as "reverse engineering" a solution.

Application

- **Mathematics**: Solving equations or word problems by isolating variables.

- **Project management**: Building timelines that begin with a fixed deadline.

- **Game strategies**: Chess endgames are analyzed by working backwards from checkmate.

- **Legal reasoning**: Lawyers build cases by working from the desired verdict to supporting evidence.

- **Escape rooms or puzzle-solving**: Players often reverse-think to unlock final steps.

Key Insights

- This heuristic is ideal when **the end state is clearly defined**, but the starting point is uncertain or overwhelming.

- It promotes **efficiency and logical clarity**, reducing trial-and-error approaches.

- It helps uncover **intermediate goals and decision points** that may be less visible in forward reasoning.

- While powerful, it requires the solver to **accurately envision the final state**—which may be challenging in abstract or ambiguous problems.

In essence, the working backwards heuristic shows that sometimes the **fastest way forward is to start at the end.**

84. Substitution heuristic

The *Substitution Heuristic* is a cognitive shortcut in which individuals unconsciously replace a complex, difficult-to-answer question with a simpler, more easily accessible one—then answer that instead. This often occurs without the individual realizing that the substitution has taken place. The concept was formalized by psychologist **Daniel Kahneman**, who observed that when people are faced with tough evaluative questions, they intuitively and quickly substitute a related, but easier, question.

This heuristic is not a deliberate deception, but a **mechanism for dealing with cognitive overload or ambiguity**. It is a key feature of *System 1* thinking (fast, automatic, intuitive) in Kahneman's dual-process model of the mind. While it often leads to plausible responses, it can also result in biased or irrational judgments.

Example

Suppose you're asked, "How happy are you with your life right now?" That's a broad, abstract question requiring deep reflection. Instead, you might unconsciously substitute an easier question like, "What's my mood right now?" and base your answer on that. If you just received good news, you might rate your life as highly satisfying—even if nothing fundamental has changed.

Another example: when asked, "How likely is this politician to succeed in office?" people might substitute, "How charismatic or confident do they seem?"—judging based on presentation rather than policy competence.

Why It Works

The substitution heuristic works because it **conserves mental effort**. Human cognition tends to favour efficiency over accuracy, especially under time pressure or information scarcity. Substitution allows the brain to **generate an answer quickly** using readily available affective or intuitive cues rather than engaging in slower, more effortful reasoning.

This trade-off is often effective in everyday life, where decisions must be made rapidly and where perfect accuracy isn't necessary. However, it becomes problematic when the substituted question leads to **systematic errors** in judgment.

How It Works

1. A complex question is posed that requires detailed analysis.

2. The brain, detecting difficulty or ambiguity, **automatically replaces** it with a simpler, related question.

3. The individual then provides an answer to the simpler question **as if it were an answer to the original one**.

4. The process is usually **unconscious**, and the individual feels confident in their response.

Application

- **Marketing**: Consumers may judge product quality based on packaging or branding (easy cues) instead of actual product performance.

- **Hiring decisions**: Interviewers may judge candidate competence based on likeability or appearance.

- **Political behaviour**: Voters may assess a candidate's effectiveness based on confidence or familiarity, not policy knowledge.

- **Risk assessment**: People often assess the danger of something (e.g., flying) based on how easily they can recall dramatic incidents, substituting vividness for probability.

Key Insights

- Substitution enables **quick decision-making** but often introduces **bias**.

- It explains many common **judgment errors**, including affect heuristic, halo effect, and representativeness.

- People are often **unaware** that they've answered a different question than the one posed.

- Recognizing when substitution is likely can help in **improving critical thinking** and **question design** (e.g., in surveys or assessments).

In essence, the substitution heuristic shows how our minds often answer the question **we can answer**, not necessarily the one **we were asked**.

85. Use of analogies heuristic

The *Use of Analogies Heuristic* is a problem-solving and decision-making strategy that involves applying knowledge from a familiar situation (the source) to a novel or unfamiliar situation (the target) by recognizing underlying similarities. Rather than reasoning from scratch, individuals draw on analogies—comparisons based on structure or relationships—to understand problems, generate solutions, or make judgments. This heuristic is grounded in **cognitive psychology** and plays a central role in **learning, creativity, and reasoning**.

Analogical thinking allows the brain to **transfer insights across domains**, reducing cognitive load and enabling fast adaptation. It's used both consciously (e.g., in deliberate teaching or explanation) and unconsciously (e.g., in intuitive reasoning).

Example

Consider a doctor diagnosing a rare disease. If the symptoms resemble a more common illness they've treated before, they may reason, "This is like case X—so treatment Y might work here too." They aren't starting from scratch; they're using a familiar framework to reason about an unfamiliar problem.

In everyday life, a manager facing team conflict might recall how they resolved a similar issue in a previous job and apply the same negotiation approach. The new problem may differ in context but share a **relational pattern**—thus, the analogy provides a usable solution.

Why It Works

Analogical reasoning works because it leverages the brain's natural **pattern recognition abilities**. It simplifies complex, unfamiliar problems by framing them in terms of something already understood. This conserves cognitive energy and accelerates decision-making, particularly in environments where information is incomplete, time is limited, or experience is scarce.

Moreover, analogies help **bridge knowledge gaps** and facilitate learning by making abstract or complex ideas more concrete and relatable.

How It Works

1. An unfamiliar problem or situation arises.

2. The mind **retrieves a known scenario** with similar structure or relational dynamics.

3. Key elements and relationships from the known case are **mapped onto the new one**.

4. A solution, interpretation, or action is generated based on that mapping.

5. The analogy may be tested, refined, or replaced as needed.

Effective analogies rely on **structural similarity**, not just superficial features. Poor analogies can mislead if critical differences are ignored.

Application

- **Education**: Teachers use analogies (e.g., comparing electrical circuits to water flow) to explain abstract concepts.

- **Law**: Legal reasoning often depends on precedent— analogous past cases to guide current decisions.

- **Entrepreneurship**: Founders compare their startup challenges to those of established companies to model strategy.

- **Science and innovation**: Breakthroughs often stem from cross-domain analogies (e.g., Darwin's natural selection inspired by artificial breeding).

- **Therapy and coaching**: Metaphors and analogies help clients reframe personal challenges.

Key Insights

- Analogies **reduce cognitive effort** and speed up problem-solving.

- They are particularly powerful for **transfer of learning** and cross-domain innovation.

- The best analogies reveal **deep structural parallels**, not surface-level similarities.

- Misleading analogies can lead to **faulty reasoning**, so discernment is crucial.

- Encouraging analogical thinking improves creativity, adaptability, and strategic insight.

In essence, the analogy heuristic highlights that **sometimes the best way to understand something new is by comparing it to something you already know**.

86. Heuristic simplification

Heuristic simplification is a mental strategy in which individuals reduce the complexity of a problem, decision, or situation by focusing only on the most salient, relevant, or manageable elements—often at the expense of completeness or precision. Rather than attempting a comprehensive analysis, people simplify by using **rules of thumb, key cues, or narrowed framing**. The core idea is: if a decision or problem feels overwhelming, simplify it until it's **good enough to act on**.

This heuristic is a response to the limitations of human cognition—particularly **bounded rationality**, as described by Herbert Simon. We have limited time, memory, and computational capacity, so simplification allows us to function effectively in a world that often exceeds our ability to process all available information.

Example

Imagine a person choosing a smartphone. Faced with dozens of brands, models, specs, and price points, they may simplify the decision by focusing only on one or two features that matter most to them—say, battery life and camera quality. Rather than comparing all 20 options across 10 dimensions, they look for the best-rated phone in just those two areas and make their choice. This is a form of heuristic simplification: reducing a multidimensional decision into a **tractable subset** of factors.

In a professional context, a manager assessing job candidates might simplify by focusing primarily on prior job titles or degrees, ignoring other qualitative factors like adaptability or teamwork.

Why It Works

Heuristic simplification works because it enables **faster, more confident decisions** under time pressure or uncertainty. Simplification **conserves cognitive resources**, reduces stress, and helps avoid decision paralysis. In many real-world situations, over-analysis can be just as risky as under-analysis—so simplifying the problem increases decisiveness and responsiveness.

It also mirrors how the brain naturally prefers **cognitive economy**—seeking patterns and key signals rather than complete information processing.

How It Works

1. The individual encounters a complex or ambiguous situation.

2. They identify or select **a few relevant dimensions**, criteria, or cues.

3. They ignore or minimize less relevant or harder-to-process information.

4. A decision or solution is formed based on the simplified model.

This often involves **truncating the decision tree**, collapsing variables, or using binary logic (e.g., yes/no, good/bad).

Application

- **Consumer decisions**: Shoppers simplify product choices by relying on brand recognition or a single key feature.

- **Medical diagnostics**: Physicians may initially simplify symptoms to common patterns to rule out major risks.

- **Project management**: Breaking down complex tasks into milestones, or prioritizing the most urgent blockers.

- **UX design**: Interfaces are designed to minimize options, guiding users toward simplified choices.

Key Insights

- Heuristic simplification is essential for **navigating complexity** but comes with trade-offs.

- It promotes **efficiency over thoroughness**, which can be advantageous or risky, depending on the context.

- Over-simplification may lead to **bias, error, or neglect of critical information**.

- Encouraging flexible simplification (e.g., knowing when to zoom in or out) improves decision quality.

- It is especially effective in high-stakes environments where **action beats perfection**.

In essence, heuristic simplification shows that **less can be more— if you simplify the right way, at the right time.**

87. Rule chaining heuristic

Rule chaining is a heuristic method used in reasoning and problem-solving where conclusions are derived by sequentially applying a set of conditional "if-then" rules. Rather than evaluating all information simultaneously, this method involves **linking rules together step-by-step**, using the output of one rule as the input for the next. It is particularly prevalent in **expert systems, artificial intelligence, and formal logic**, and mirrors how people often reason in everyday tasks: by building arguments or deductions one step at a time.

There are two primary forms of rule chaining:

- **Forward chaining**: Starts with known facts and applies rules to infer new facts, progressing toward a goal.

- **Backward chaining**: Starts with a goal and works backward to see if the goal can be satisfied by existing rules and facts.

This chaining approach allows complex reasoning to unfold from **a series of simple, understandable steps**, promoting clarity, modularity, and scalability.

Example

Consider a medical diagnostic expert system. It might apply the following rule chain:

1. If a patient has a fever and cough, then suspect infection.

2. If an infection is suspected and white blood cell count is high, then bacterial infection is likely.

3. If bacterial infection is likely, then recommend antibiotics.

Each rule is applied sequentially, with the conclusion of one feeding into the condition of the next. A physician or system can thus **derive a diagnosis and treatment recommendation** by chaining together these logical steps.

In everyday life, a person might think: "If it's raining, I'll need an umbrella. If I need an umbrella, I should check the hallway. If the hallway doesn't have it, I'll go to the car." This casual form of rule chaining helps manage sequential decisions under practical constraints.

Why It Works

Rule chaining works because it **organizes knowledge in modular, reusable components**, allowing complex reasoning to be broken down into manageable logical steps. It's especially effective in structured environments where conditions and consequences are clearly defined. This heuristic also reduces errors by ensuring that each step follows logically from the previous, supporting traceability and explanation.

It aligns well with how human cognition often operates—through **linear sequences of cause-effect associations**.

How It Works

1. The system or person identifies initial facts or a goal.

2. A rule is triggered when its conditions match the current state.

3. The rule's outcome is added to the knowledge base or used as a new subgoal.

4. The process continues until a goal is reached (forward) or validated (backward).

5. The chain can then be reviewed or revised as needed.

This iterative, modular reasoning structure mirrors programming logic and diagnostic frameworks.

Application

- **AI and expert systems**: Diagnosing problems in medicine, engineering, or IT.

- **Legal reasoning**: Applying statutes in sequential logic to determine case outcomes.

- **Education**: Teaching logic or grammar rules step-by-step.

- **Robotics**: Programming reactive behaviour in rule-based environments.

- **Game design**: Decision trees and AI behaviours often use rule chains.

Key Insights

- Rule chaining promotes **structured reasoning**, especially where cause-and-effect logic applies.

- It enhances **transparency and traceability**, making decisions easier to audit or explain.

- The method excels in domains with **formalized knowledge**, but may struggle with ambiguity or incomplete rules.

- Rule chaining can be **forward-driven (data-focused)** or **goal-driven (objective-focused)** depending on context.

- The quality of outcomes depends heavily on **rule accuracy, completeness, and logical consistency**.

In essence, rule chaining illustrates how **complex decisions often emerge from a series of simple, connected steps**—one rule at a time.

88. Chunking heuristic

Chunking is a cognitive heuristic that involves grouping individual pieces of information into larger, meaningful units—or "chunks"—to enhance memory, understanding, and problem-solving efficiency. Rather than processing data as isolated elements, the brain compresses it into more manageable patterns or categories. This heuristic is foundational in **cognitive psychology**, particularly in studies of **working memory** and **expert performance**.

The chunking concept was notably explored by psychologist **George A. Miller** in his influential 1956 paper *"The Magical Number Seven, Plus or Minus Two,"* which proposed that people can hold about 7 (±2) items in their short-term memory at once. Chunking helps extend this limit by **recoding information into meaningful clusters**, making it easier to store and retrieve.

Example

Consider trying to memorize this sequence: 1-4-9-2-1-7-7-6. At first glance, it appears as eight random digits. However, if you recognize and group it as two historical years—1492 (Columbus's voyage) and 1776 (U.S. Declaration of Independence)—you've reduced eight items into **two meaningful chunks**.

Similarly, a chess master doesn't see a random configuration of pieces but meaningful patterns such as "fianchettoed bishop" or "castled kingside." These chunks allow them to process and recall vast board configurations far more efficiently than a novice.

Why It Works

Chunking works because it **reduces cognitive load** by taking advantage of patterns, familiarity, and prior knowledge. Our brains are not optimized for raw data storage but for organizing information into **schemas** and **structures**. By chunking, we bypass the raw capacity limits of working memory, enabling us to work with more complex data in a shorter time frame.

It also facilitates **long-term memory encoding** by linking new information to existing knowledge frameworks.

How It Works

1. **Identify relationships or patterns** within information (e.g., similarities, sequences, categories).

2. **Group related elements** into a single, larger unit (the chunk).

3. Use the chunk as a single cognitive unit during recall or problem-solving.

4. With repeated exposure, chunks become **automatic and more abstract**, allowing for increasingly efficient thinking.

Chunking can be improved with practice and is **highly dependent on prior knowledge**—the more familiar the material, the more effective the chunking.

Application

- **Education**: Students use chunking to memorize vocabulary, formulas, or historical dates.

- **Programming**: Developers chunk lines of code into functional blocks or reusable components.

- **Athletics**: Athletes learn complex plays or movements as grouped routines rather than isolated actions.

- **Language learning**: Phrases are learned in chunks (e.g., "Nice to meet you") instead of word-by-word.

- **Interface design**: Grouping buttons or tasks visually helps users navigate systems intuitively.

Key Insights

- Chunking is a **powerful strategy for overcoming memory limitations**.

- It relies on the **recognition of patterns or meaning**, not just compression of data.

- Experts in any domain chunk more efficiently than novices, which explains superior performance.

- Effective chunking requires **contextual understanding**, so teaching should emphasize structure and relevance.

- The strategy improves both **recall speed and problem-solving capacity**.

In essence, chunking shows that **how we organize information matters just as much as the information itself**.

89. Divide big problem into small problems heuristic

The *Divide Big Problem into Small Problems* heuristic—also known as *decomposition* or *problem partitioning*—involves breaking down a complex, overwhelming task into smaller, more manageable sub-problems. Rather than attempting to solve a large problem in one step, this strategy allows individuals to focus on solving one component at a time, which cumulatively leads to a solution for the larger issue. It is widely used in fields ranging from mathematics and computer science to project management and personal productivity.

This heuristic is closely related to the concept of **"divide and conquer"** in algorithm design and to **chunking** in cognitive psychology. It aligns with the human brain's preference for simplicity, structure, and progression. Tackling smaller units makes the problem appear less intimidating, enabling better focus and progress tracking.

Example

Imagine you're tasked with writing a 20-page research report. If approached as one massive undertaking, the task can seem paralyzing. Using this heuristic, you might break the task into smaller steps: choosing a topic, conducting initial research, outlining the structure, writing each section (introduction, literature review, methodology, etc.), and revising. Each sub-task has its own goal, making the overall process more digestible and trackable.

Similarly, in software development, building a full application is broken into front-end, back-end, database design, and testing— each of which can be tackled independently and then integrated.

Why It Works

This heuristic works because it **reduces cognitive overload**. Humans have limited attention spans and working memory, and attempting to juggle too many aspects of a large problem can lead to anxiety or paralysis. By focusing on smaller, well-defined problems, individuals can engage in **deep, focused work** and experience a sense of accomplishment from each solved piece. This promotes **motivation and momentum**.

Psychologically, completing sub-tasks also offers small wins, which release dopamine, reinforcing motivation to continue working.

How It Works

1. **Define the overall goal** or problem.

2. **Break it down into logical sub-tasks or components**.

3. Prioritize or sequence the smaller problems.

4. **Solve each sub-problem individually**, monitoring progress.

5. **Integrate the solutions** to construct the complete solution.

This can be recursive—some sub-problems may themselves be broken down further.

Application

- **Education**: Breaking a complex subject (e.g., calculus) into foundational units (limits, derivatives, integrals).

- **Business strategy**: Dividing a strategic goal (e.g., market expansion) into target research, logistics, marketing, and sales components.

- **Software development**: Modular coding enables parallel development and easier debugging.

- **Personal productivity**: Managing tasks through daily to-dos, timelines, or habit trackers.

- **Engineering**: Large construction projects are broken into site preparation, structural work, electrical, plumbing, etc.

Key Insights

- Decomposition fosters **clarity, organization, and efficiency**.

- It aligns with how the brain prefers to solve problems— **one bite at a time**.

- Enables **parallel work**, especially in teams.

- Encourages iterative improvement and **early detection of issues**.

- Not all problems divide cleanly—some require careful identification of interdependencies.

In essence, this heuristic shows that **solving the whole often starts by solving the parts**—making progress possible through structure and focus.

90. "If it works, don't fix it" heuristic

The *"If it works, don't fix it"* heuristic is a practical decision-making rule that encourages individuals or systems to maintain the status quo when something is functioning adequately, even if it is not optimal. Instead of attempting to tweak, redesign, or improve a process or solution that is already yielding acceptable results, this heuristic suggests conserving effort, avoiding unnecessary change, and minimizing the risk of unintended consequences.

Rooted in **conservatism bias** and **satisficing**, this rule reflects the logic of **efficiency and risk aversion**: resources such as time, energy, and money should not be spent reinventing functioning processes unless there is a clear need. It's commonly seen in engineering, business operations, and day-to-day life.

Example

Imagine a company using an old inventory management system. It's not cutting-edge, but it handles orders accurately, staff are familiar with it, and operations flow smoothly. A proposal is made to upgrade the system to something more modern. However, leadership hesitates. Their reasoning: "The current system works. It may be outdated, but it meets our needs, and changing it could cause disruption or introduce new bugs."

This is a textbook use of the "If it works, don't fix it" heuristic—opting for continuity over innovation in the absence of pressing problems.

Why It Works

This heuristic works because it **prioritizes stability and minimizes risk**. Many real-world systems—especially in healthcare, aviation, or IT infrastructure—are finely balanced. Tinkering with them without a compelling reason may introduce vulnerabilities. Moreover, humans have limited cognitive and operational resources. Constantly chasing improvements can lead to **diminishing returns**, burnout, or "optimization paralysis."

Additionally, it aligns with the **Pareto Principle**—80% of the benefits often come from 20% of the system. Chasing the last 20% may not be worth the effort or risk.

How It Works

1. A solution or process is assessed to determine if it **meets performance criteria**.

2. If the outcome is acceptable (though not necessarily ideal), no changes are made.

3. Efforts are redirected to areas of **greater need or higher potential return**.

4. Re-evaluation only occurs when issues emerge or external conditions change.

This approach acts as a filter, preventing unnecessary intervention or overengineering.

Application

- **Engineering**: Legacy code is often left untouched if it's stable and critical.

- **Healthcare**: Stable treatment protocols are not changed without evidence of superior alternatives.

- **Business processes**: Functional workflows are maintained until a clear inefficiency appears.

- **Product design**: Well-functioning features remain unchanged across versions to preserve user familiarity.

Key Insights

- This heuristic conserves **effort, reduces risk, and prevents disruption**.

- It is not anti-improvement but **pro-stability**, assuming no significant problems exist.

- It aligns with the philosophy of **"satisficing"**—settling for "good enough" when it's cost-effective.

- Caution: it may **stifle innovation** or lead to complacency if applied dogmatically.

- Best used in **stable environments** where reliability outweighs marginal gains.

In essence, the "If it works, don't fix it" heuristic underscores that **progress doesn't always mean change—sometimes, success lies in knowing when not to act.**

⟳ **Learning & Memory Heuristics**

91. Spaced repetition heuristic

The *Spaced Repetition Heuristic* is a cognitive learning strategy based on the insight that information is more effectively retained in long-term memory when it is reviewed at increasing intervals over time. Rather than cramming or reviewing material in massed sessions, spaced repetition spreads out study sessions so that each review occurs just as the learner is on the verge of forgetting the material—a point known as the *optimal retrieval interval*.

This heuristic is grounded in the **spacing effect**, a psychological phenomenon first identified by **Hermann Ebbinghaus** in the late 19th century. Ebbinghaus' research on memory revealed that the brain retains information better when exposure to that information is spaced out rather than concentrated in one session. Spaced repetition thus leverages **forgetting as a tool for stronger retention**.

Example

Imagine someone learning a new language. If they encounter a new vocabulary word—say, *"libro"* (Spanish for "book")—they might review it on Day 1, again on Day 3, then on Day 7, and later on Day 14. If they recall the word each time, the interval before the next review lengthens. If they forget, the interval shortens.

Over time, the word moves into long-term memory with far fewer repetitions than traditional rote memorization would require.

Modern applications include tools like **Anki** or **Quizlet**, which use algorithms to calculate optimal review times based on user performance.

Why It Works

Spaced repetition works because it aligns with how memory functions: **retrieval strengthens memory**, especially when it's slightly effortful. When information is reviewed just as it's about to be forgotten, the act of recalling it **reinforces the memory trace**, making future recall easier and more durable.

This heuristic also helps to avoid the illusion of mastery—a common problem with cramming—by distributing learning over time and introducing desirable difficulty.

How It Works

1. A learner studies new information.

2. The information is reviewed at **increasing intervals**, depending on retention strength.

3. Each successful recall **resets or lengthens the interval**.

4. Forgotten items are reviewed more frequently.

5. Over time, well-learned material requires less review, freeing up cognitive resources.

Many systems use **spaced algorithms** that adjust intervals dynamically, personalizing the experience for each learner.

Application

- **Education**: Flashcard systems and adaptive learning platforms for vocabulary, formulas, or historical facts.

- **Medical training**: Physicians and students retain complex procedures or terminology using spaced repetition apps.

- **Test preparation**: GRE, MCAT, and language learners benefit from regular, spaced reviews.

- **Corporate training**: Microlearning modules spaced out improve compliance and retention in workplace education.

- **Self-improvement**: Habit tracking and knowledge journaling are enhanced through spaced reflection.

Key Insights

- Spaced repetition is a **highly efficient learning strategy**, enabling long-term retention with less total study time.

- It encourages **active recall**, which is more effective than passive review.

- The technique reduces **cognitive fatigue and information overload**.

- It turns **forgetting into a trigger** for learning, rather than a failure.

- Requires planning or technological support to manage intervals effectively.

In essence, the Spaced Repetition Heuristic shows that **the best way to remember more is to study less—but smarter and at the right time**.

92. Retrieval fluency heuristic

The *Retrieval Fluency Heuristic* is a cognitive shortcut where individuals judge the likelihood, frequency, or importance of something based on how easily instances or information come to mind. The more fluently something can be recalled—whether due to familiarity, recent exposure, or vividness—the more significant or frequent it is perceived to be. This heuristic is closely related to the **availability heuristic** but focuses more narrowly on **the ease of recall** rather than just the quantity of recalled items.

Retrieval fluency plays a vital role in **decision-making, judgments, and perception**, especially when individuals must make quick estimations without thorough data analysis. In cognitive psychology, fluency is considered a *meta-cognitive cue*—a feeling or signal that the brain uses to assess how much it "knows" something.

Example

Imagine someone asked to estimate which city has more crime: Chicago or St. Louis. If that person has recently seen multiple news stories about shootings in Chicago, the name "Chicago" may come to mind more easily, leading them to overestimate its crime rate—even if statistics show otherwise. The speed and ease with which examples of crime in Chicago are recalled make it seem riskier.

In another context, when asked to list reasons why a job is enjoyable, people who can quickly name several reasons may rate their job satisfaction higher than those who struggle—even if both groups name the same total number of reasons eventually.

Why It Works

Retrieval fluency works because the brain tends to equate **ease with truth**. If something is easy to recall, it's assumed to be common, important, or correct. This stems from an evolutionary efficiency: when rapid decisions were necessary for survival, relying on what readily came to mind helped facilitate quick actions.

Additionally, fluency often correlates with real-world frequency or relevance—though not always—making it a **generally effective but imperfect proxy** for decision-making.

How It Works

1. A person is asked to make a judgment or decision based on memory.

2. They search for relevant examples, data, or concepts.

3. The **speed and effort of recall** influence the judgment.

4. If information is retrieved **fluently (quickly, smoothly)**, it is seen as more true, likely, or important.

5. Conversely, difficulty in retrieval may cause underestimation or doubt.

Fluency can be influenced by **priming, repetition, familiarity, vividness, and even font readability**.

Application

- **Marketing**: Brands strive for repeated exposure so their names are more easily recalled (fluency boosts preference).

- **Education**: Students judge how well they've learned based on how easily they recall concepts—though this can mislead.

- **Legal reasoning**: Jurors may overvalue vivid testimonies or easily recalled evidence.

- **Investing**: Stocks in the news feel "safer" or "riskier" depending on recent memory associations.

- **Health behaviour**: Risks that are easier to recall (like plane crashes) feel more probable than statistically frequent but less vivid dangers (like heart disease).

Key Insights

- Retrieval fluency can **skew judgments** even when memory content is accurate.

- It reflects a **fast, intuitive process** used when data is lacking or incomplete.

- Fluency can be **manipulated by media, design, or repetition**, making it a tool for persuasion.

- Over-reliance can lead to **bias**, especially when fluency stems from irrelevant factors (e.g., font clarity or emotion).

In essence, the Retrieval Fluency Heuristic reveals that **what comes to mind easily often seems more true—even if it isn't.**

93. Heuristic cue association

Heuristic Cue Association refers to a mental shortcut where individuals make judgments or decisions based on the presence of **surface-level cues** that are associated with deeper meanings or outcomes. Instead of engaging in detailed evaluation, people rely on certain features—like appearance, labels, tone, or symbols—that act as **mental triggers** for specific inferences. These cues are learned through experience, culture, or repeated exposure, and they operate below conscious awareness much of the time.

This heuristic draws from **associative learning theory** and **cue-based processing**, where patterns of co-occurrence (e.g., a doctor's white coat with competence) become internalized. Over time, the presence of a familiar cue (e.g., a confident tone) becomes a **proxy for a more complex judgment** (e.g., credibility).

Example

Imagine you're shopping for wine and you see two bottles: one has a French-sounding name with a gold-embossed label, and the other has a plain, unfamiliar brand. You instinctively choose the fancier-looking one, assuming it's higher quality. Here, the **label design and name** act as heuristic cues. You haven't tasted the wine or reviewed any data, but your decision is guided by associative cues linked with quality.

Another example: a person hears a political figure speak in an authoritative tone, wearing a suit, and standing in front of a flag. These cues—tone, attire, setting—can unconsciously lead the listener to assume legitimacy or competence, regardless of the actual content being delivered.

Why It Works

Heuristic cue association works because it allows the brain to make **fast, efficient decisions** in situations where full analysis would be too slow or cognitively demanding. These cues are often based on **real patterns**—certain appearances or behaviours *do* tend to align with particular traits—but they can also be misleading or exploited.

Moreover, cues often trigger **emotional or intuitive responses**, making them especially persuasive in social or commercial contexts.

How It Works

- A cue (visual, auditory, linguistic, etc.) is detected.

- The cue activates **associated concepts or evaluations** based on past experience.

- The brain **uses the association as a substitute** for deeper reasoning.

- A judgment or choice is made, typically with confidence and speed.

This heuristic is **non-analytic**—meaning it bypasses conscious deliberation and relies on pattern recognition and stored associations.

Application

- **Marketing**: Use of colour, fonts, slogans, and celebrity endorsements are designed to evoke automatic associations with quality, trust, or style.

- **Politics**: Flags, podiums, formal dress, and crowd reactions signal authority and legitimacy.

- **Hiring**: A well-dressed, confident candidate might be perceived as more competent based on visual cues.

- **Education**: Students may infer the difficulty of a subject from how it's presented—dense text or complex graphs may cue "hard subject."

Key Insights

- Heuristic cue association **enables speed but risks bias**.

- It operates **unconsciously**, which makes it powerful—and manipulable.

- Cues are **learned** and **context-dependent**, and can vary across cultures.

- While often effective, this heuristic can lead to **stereotyping, superficial judgments**, or brand misperceptions.

- Increasing awareness of cues allows for **better critical thinking** and helps resist manipulation.

In essence, this heuristic shows that **how something looks, sounds, or feels often shapes what we believe about it—long before we think it through.**

94. Mnemonic heuristics

Mnemonic heuristics are cognitive shortcuts that help individuals encode, retain, and retrieve information by associating it with more memorable patterns, phrases, or structures. These heuristics leverage **meaningful associations**, such as acronyms, rhymes, imagery, or chunking, to transform abstract or arbitrary information into something easier to recall. Rather than relying on rote memorization, mnemonic techniques utilize existing cognitive strengths—like rhythm, spatial memory, or narrative—to facilitate **efficient recall**.

The term "mnemonic" stems from the Greek word *mnēmē*, meaning memory. These strategies are especially powerful in educational contexts and are rooted in **cognitive psychology**, particularly in the domain of **encoding specificity and elaborative rehearsal**. Mnemonics function by linking new information to something already well-represented in long-term memory.

Example

A well-known example is the acronym **ROY G. BIV**, used to remember the colours of the visible spectrum in order: Red, Orange, Yellow, Green, Blue, Indigo, Violet. Each letter represents a colour, and the phrase gives structure to an otherwise random sequence.

Another is **"Please Excuse My Dear Aunt Sally"**—a mnemonic to remember the order of operations in math: Parentheses, Exponents, Multiplication, Division, Addition, Subtraction. By embedding the rules into a sentence, students find it much easier to retrieve the sequence under pressure.

Why It Works

Mnemonic heuristics work because they help overcome the **limitations of working memory** by embedding new data into **meaningful, often visual or auditory structures**. They exploit how the brain naturally prefers **patterns, stories, and emotional cues** over arbitrary data.

This heuristic also leverages **dual coding theory**—information is more easily remembered when encoded both verbally and visually—and the **depth of processing theory**, which states that the more deeply we process information, the better we retain it. Mnemonics require the learner to engage in elaboration, creating deeper mental connections.

How It Works

1. Identify information that is difficult to remember as-is.

2. Transform it into a structured or symbolic form (acronym, image, rhyme, etc.).

3. Associate the mnemonic with the target content.

4. Use repetition and visualization to reinforce the association.

5. Retrieve the mnemonic to access the original information.

Over time, the mnemonic becomes a reliable cue for deeper recall.

Application

-   **Education**: Students use mnemonics to memorize lists, equations, historical dates, and biological classifications.

-   **Medical training**: Medical professionals rely on mnemonics like **"SOAP"** for patient notes: Subjective, Objective, Assessment, Plan.

-   **Language learning**: Associating foreign vocabulary with vivid images or sounds.

-   **Public safety**: Mnemonics like **"STOP, DROP, and ROLL"** help instill quick behavioural responses.

-   **Everyday life**: Remembering passwords, grocery lists, or directions through rhymes or patterns.

Key Insights

-   Mnemonics are **fast, effective tools** for improving memory and retrieval.

- They help bridge **short-term and long-term memory** by creating strong associations.

- The more **personally meaningful or vivid** the mnemonic, the more powerful its effect.

- Mnemonic use enhances **confidence and fluency**, especially in high-stress recall situations.

- However, they may oversimplify content and are best used in **conjunction with deeper learning**.

In essence, mnemonic heuristics demonstrate that **memory is not just about repetition—but about transformation.**

95. "Testing effect" heuristic

The *Testing Effect* is a learning and memory heuristic where retrieving information through testing leads to **better long-term retention** than simply re-studying the material. Contrary to the common belief that tests only assess knowledge, this heuristic reveals that the act of being tested itself **enhances learning**. This effect has been widely supported in cognitive psychology, particularly in the work of researchers like Henry Roediger and Jeffrey Karpicke.

Rather than viewing testing as a passive checkpoint, the testing effect redefines it as an **active learning strategy**. The effort of recalling information strengthens neural pathways and embeds knowledge more deeply into long-term memory. This heuristic highlights retrieval as not just a consequence of learning, but a *mechanism for learning*.

Example

Imagine two students preparing for a history exam. Student A reads the textbook multiple times. Student B reads it once, then uses flashcards to quiz herself on the material. On test day, Student B performs significantly better. Even though she studied less overall, the process of **actively retrieving information** helped solidify it in her memory more effectively than repeated reading did for Student A.

This applies beyond academic settings. For instance, a firefighter regularly engages in drills where they mentally rehearse procedures and recall safety protocols under simulated pressure. When real emergencies arise, their memory is sharper and faster due to consistent testing and retrieval practice.

Why It Works

The testing effect works because **retrieval strengthens memory**. When we recall information, we reactivate and reconsolidate memory traces, making them more durable and easier to access in the future. This process encourages **deep encoding**, forces attention, and highlights knowledge gaps, guiding more efficient review.

Additionally, the difficulty and effort involved in recall—referred to as **desirable difficulty**—enhances learning far more than passive review. It's not just repetition, but **effortful engagement** that drives mastery.

How It Works

1. Learn new material through reading, listening, or observation.

2. Instead of only re-reading, **actively retrieve** the information via quizzes, practice questions, or self-testing.

3. Use feedback to identify and correct errors, strengthening correct knowledge.

4. Space out retrieval attempts (combining with **spaced repetition**) for optimal reinforcement.

This heuristic can be applied to both simple fact-based learning and complex conceptual understanding.

Application

- **Education**: Students benefit from low-stakes quizzes, flashcards, and retrieval-based study tools like Anki.

- **Professional training**: Pilot simulations, medical case reviews, and military drills all enhance retention via recall.

- **Self-study**: Journaling what you remember from a lecture or book instead of re-reading it.

- **Language learning**: Testing vocabulary through self-quizzing rather than passive reading.

Key Insights

- Retrieval isn't just assessment—it's an **active enhancer of memory**.

- Frequent, low-stakes testing builds **confidence and fluency** over time.

- Combining the testing effect with **spaced repetition** and **feedback loops** supercharges learning.

- Learners often underestimate its value, assuming rereading is enough—yet testing is *far more effective*.

- The benefit grows over time: **testing helps retain knowledge long after it's first learned**.

In essence, the testing effect shows that **to remember better, you must practice remembering.**

96. Context-dependent recall heuristic

Context-dependent recall is a memory heuristic where information is more easily retrieved when the context at the time of recall **matches the context** present during initial learning or encoding. In other words, the physical, emotional, or situational environment in which a memory was formed becomes a cue for recalling that memory later. This phenomenon supports the idea that memory is not stored in isolation but is **embedded within a web of contextual details**.

This heuristic is based on **encoding specificity theory**, introduced by cognitive psychologists Endel Tulving and Donald Thomson. According to this theory, memory is most effectively retrieved when contextual cues available at encoding are reinstated at retrieval. The brain stores not just the information, but also the background environment, emotional state, and sensory cues present during learning.

Example

A famous experiment by Godden and Baddeley (1975) illustrates this well. Scuba divers learned a list of words either underwater or on land. Later, they were asked to recall the words in either the same or different environment. Results showed that divers who recalled the words in the **same context in which they learned them (underwater or on land)** performed significantly better. The context of learning served as a memory cue, enhancing recall.

In everyday life, a student might find it easier to recall lecture content when sitting in the same classroom where it was originally taught, or someone might suddenly remember an old memory upon revisiting their childhood home.

Why It Works

Context-dependent recall works because the human brain **associates information with environmental and situational cues** during encoding. When these cues are present during recall, they trigger the associated memory networks more efficiently. This is a form of **associative learning**: the more overlap between the encoding and retrieval context, the easier it is to access stored information.

The heuristic reduces cognitive load by utilizing **external cues** to prompt internal memory retrieval, saving mental effort.

How It Works

1. During learning, the brain encodes both the **target information** and contextual details (location, smells, sounds, etc.).

2. These cues become linked in memory.

3. At the time of recall, if the context is similar, it **activates overlapping neural pathways**, facilitating memory retrieval.

4. A mismatch in context may reduce cue availability, making recall harder.

Even **internal context** (like mood or physiological state) can play a role—known as *state-dependent memory*.

Application

- **Education**: Encouraging students to study in environments similar to testing conditions improves exam performance.

- **Eyewitness testimony**: Returning to a crime scene can aid memory accuracy.

- **Workplace training**: Practicing tasks in the actual environment where they'll be performed increases retention and performance.

- **Everyday life**: Making grocery lists in the kitchen may help retrieval at the store due to overlapping context cues.

Key Insights

- Context acts as a **powerful, often unconscious retrieval aid**.

- Matching physical, emotional, or sensory environments during learning and recall boosts memory.

- This heuristic highlights the **importance of situational awareness** in memory processes.

- While helpful, over-reliance on specific contexts can limit flexible recall—generalizing across environments can be trained.

- It suggests that **learning is not just about what you study, but *where and how* you study**.

In essence, context-dependent recall shows that **where you learn shapes what you remember.**

97. First impression heuristic

The *First Impression Heuristic* refers to the cognitive shortcut in which people form lasting judgments about others based on their **initial exposure**, often within seconds. These impressions— formed from appearance, voice, body language, or initial behaviour—frequently shape future perceptions, even in the face of contradictory information. This heuristic illustrates how quickly and unconsciously the brain seeks **cognitive closure** in social situations, prioritizing early information in what's known as the **primacy effect**.

Rooted in **social cognition** and **evolutionary psychology**, this heuristic evolved as an adaptive function—quickly categorizing others as friend or foe enhanced survival. Today, it still plays a crucial role in social and professional contexts, despite its tendency to produce bias or error.

Example

Imagine you're introduced to a new colleague at work. She greets you with a firm handshake, maintains eye contact, and smiles confidently. Within seconds, you judge her as competent, trustworthy, and assertive. These positive traits may colour your ongoing interactions, making you more likely to interpret her actions favourably—even if her later performance is inconsistent. Conversely, a poor first impression—such as appearing distracted or aloof—may lead to persistent negative biases, regardless of subsequent improvements.

This heuristic explains why interviewers often make up their minds within minutes, why first dates carry disproportionate weight, and why political candidates' demeanor during debates can sway opinions.

Why It Works

The heuristic works because the brain is constantly trying to **reduce uncertainty**. In ambiguous situations, such as meeting someone new, we rely on **salient early cues** to form a mental model. These early cues—however incomplete—anchor our perceptions, shaping what we notice, remember, and believe afterward. This is a case of **anchoring bias**, where initial information unduly influences subsequent judgments.

Additionally, first impressions are often **emotionally charged** and formed under conditions of **limited information**, making them easier to recall and more resistant to change.

How It Works

1. Upon encountering a person, your brain processes visual, auditory, and behavioural cues.

2. Within milliseconds to a few seconds, you form a holistic judgment.

3. This impression acts as a **cognitive filter**—future information is interpreted through this lens.

4. Even contradictory data may be dismissed or reinterpreted to fit the original impression.

This process is largely **automatic and unconscious**, though it can be overridden with effort.

Application

- **Hiring**: Employers may unconsciously favour candidates who present themselves confidently in the first few moments.

- **Marketing**: Product packaging and branding are designed to evoke immediate trust or interest.

- **Education**: Teachers may unconsciously form expectations based on a student's demeanor on day one.

- **Politics**: Voter opinions are often swayed by first impressions during debates or speeches.

Key Insights

- First impressions are **fast, durable, and difficult to revise**.

- They rely on **incomplete data** and are vulnerable to bias (e.g., attractiveness, cultural stereotypes).

- While useful for efficiency, they can lead to **unfair or inaccurate judgments**.

- Awareness of this heuristic allows for **greater objectivity and reflection**, especially in high-stakes situations.

- It underscores the importance of **intentional presentation**, especially in introductions, interviews, and negotiations.

In essence, the First Impression Heuristic reminds us that **the beginning of any interaction often sets the tone for everything that follows—fairly or not.**

98. Recency heuristic

The *Recency Heuristic* is a cognitive shortcut in which people give disproportionate weight to the most **recent information** when making judgments, decisions, or evaluations. Instead of processing all relevant data equally, the brain privileges what has just occurred or what was last presented. This heuristic is rooted in the **recency effect**, a concept from memory research showing that items presented last in a sequence are recalled more easily than those in the middle.

From a cognitive standpoint, recent experiences are **more accessible** in memory, feel more relevant, and are often mistaken for being more important. This can streamline decision-making but also lead to **biased conclusions**, especially when recent events are anomalies or not representative of the broader context.

Example

Consider a teacher grading student presentations throughout the day. Despite trying to be fair, they may be more impressed by the last few presentations simply because those performances are freshest in memory. As a result, later presenters might receive higher marks than earlier ones, not because their content was better, but because of the **recency bias** embedded in human cognition.

Another example occurs in job interviews: candidates interviewed later in the day are often remembered more vividly and may be favoured over earlier ones with similar or even superior qualifications.

Why It Works

The recency heuristic works because of the way our **short-term memory and attention systems** operate. Recent information is more **salient, vivid, and cognitively accessible**, making it easier to retrieve and apply in decision-making. Our brain naturally assumes that what's top of mind is also **most relevant**, even when that's not objectively true.

In environments with high information load or fatigue, the brain's tendency to **"anchor" decisions on the most recent data** helps reduce cognitive strain and accelerate choices.

How It Works

1. A person encounters a series of events, items, or options.

2. The last or most recent ones remain **active in working memory**.

3. When making a decision, the brain relies on this recent input as a primary cue.

4. Earlier information is either forgotten or **overridden**, especially if not encoded deeply.

5. Judgments are formed that favour recent impressions, often unconsciously.

This mechanism is **automatic**, though it can be moderated with deliberate reflection or structured decision-making tools.

Application

- **Performance reviews**: Managers might overvalue recent employee behaviour over long-term patterns.

- **Consumer behaviour**: Shoppers may choose a brand they saw in the most recent ad, even if it's not the best option.

- **Legal judgments**: Jurors may be swayed by the order of witness testimony—favoring the last person who spoke.

- **Stock trading**: Investors often respond to the most recent market movements, ignoring long-term trends.

Key Insights

- The recency heuristic helps with **quick decision-making**, especially when attention is limited.

- It introduces **bias** when recent information is given more weight than it deserves.

- This heuristic is often **subconscious**, leading to distorted memory and evaluation.

- To counter it, individuals should consider the **entire timeline** of data, not just the final portion.

- Structured tools like checklists, scoring rubrics, or spaced reviews can reduce its negative impact.

In essence, the Recency Heuristic reminds us that **what's recent isn't always what's most important—but it often feels that way.**

99. Frequency-based heuristic

Frequency-Based Heuristic

The *Frequency-Based Heuristic* is a cognitive strategy in which individuals estimate the likelihood, truth, or importance of an event or idea based on how **frequently** they encounter it. Instead of performing complex statistical analysis or deep evaluations, the brain uses exposure frequency as a **proxy for reliability or significance**. This heuristic is rooted in **cognitive efficiency**—the brain prefers simple, fast rules that often work well enough for everyday decisions.

It operates under the assumption that if something is encountered often, it is probably true, common, or important. While this can be accurate in many real-world situations, it is also vulnerable to **distortion by repetition, media influence**, and **confirmation bias**.

Example

Suppose someone sees multiple news stories in a short time about shark attacks. Even if the statistical likelihood of such an event is extremely low, the repeated exposure leads them to believe shark attacks are far more frequent and dangerous than they actually are. As a result, they might avoid swimming in the ocean altogether.

In another example, if a student repeatedly hears that a particular major (e.g., computer science) leads to high-paying jobs, they may choose it, not because of deep personal interest or comprehensive career research, but because the message has been **frequently reinforced** in their environment.

Why It Works

The heuristic works because **frequency is often correlated with real-world regularity**. For example, hearing many people say a restaurant is good often aligns with a positive experience. Our brains are evolved to **notice patterns and regularities**—a fundamental part of learning and adaptation.

Moreover, frequent exposure increases **processing fluency**—the ease with which we recall or recognize information. This fluency is then misattributed to truth or validity, a phenomenon known as the **illusory truth effect**.

How It Works

1. A person encounters repeated messages, claims, or events.

2. The repetition increases the **availability and fluency** of the information.

3. The brain interprets this fluency as a signal of truth or importance.

4. Judgments and decisions are then formed based on **perceived frequency**, not necessarily factual evidence.

This process is largely **automatic and unconscious**, influenced by memory, exposure, and pattern recognition.

Application

- **Advertising**: Brands use repeated messaging to build familiarity, which increases consumer trust and preference.

- **Politics**: Campaign slogans and repeated claims—true or false—can shape public opinion through sheer repetition.

- **Social media**: Viral content is often seen as more valid or valuable simply because it appears frequently.

- **Education**: Repeated exposure to key concepts aids in retention and influences perceived importance.

- **Health communication**: Repetition of health warnings increases awareness and behaviour change (e.g., anti-smoking campaigns).

Key Insights

- The frequency-based heuristic is **efficient and often accurate**, but it can be manipulated.

- Repetition can **create the illusion of truth**, even in the absence of evidence.

- It highlights the **power of exposure** in shaping beliefs, preferences, and behaviours.

- Recognizing this heuristic can help people **guard against misinformation** and become more critical consumers of information.

- Frequency alone shouldn't substitute for **fact-checking, reasoning, or diverse perspectives**.

In essence, the Frequency-Based Heuristic reveals that **what we see often, we tend to believe—even when we shouldn't.**

100. Serial position heuristic

Serial Position Heuristic

The *Serial Position Heuristic* is a cognitive shortcut in which individuals tend to remember and give greater weight to information presented at the **beginning** (primacy effect) and the **end** (recency effect) of a sequence, while often overlooking the middle. This heuristic is deeply rooted in the way **human memory processes sequential information**, and it explains why the order of information presentation can dramatically affect what we remember and how we evaluate it.

This phenomenon arises from the **serial position effect**, first demonstrated by Hermann Ebbinghaus and later expanded by researchers in cognitive psychology. The heuristic is particularly influential in decision-making, communication, and learning, as people often base their choices not on the full set of information, but on what stood out **at the start and end.**

Example

Consider a job interview where a panel sees ten candidates in one day. The first candidate makes a strong, memorable impression, and the last candidate presents with clarity and confidence. Even if candidates in the middle were equally or more qualified, the first and last are more likely to be recalled favourably. This is a practical demonstration of the serial position heuristic influencing decision-making.

In marketing, product ads shown first and last in a sequence (like during commercial breaks or scrolling through a list) are remembered more, and thus more likely to influence consumer behaviour.

Why It Works

The serial position heuristic works because of how information is processed and stored in **short-term and long-term memory**. Items presented first benefit from extra rehearsal time and deeper processing, becoming anchored in long-term memory (primacy). Meanwhile, items presented last are still present in short-term or working memory at the time of recall (recency), making them easier to retrieve.

This cognitive tendency allows the brain to focus on salient information without having to process every item in detail—an efficient, though sometimes flawed, way to deal with information overload.

How It Works

1. A person is presented with a sequence of items, ideas, or options.

2. The **first few items** receive more attention and rehearsal, embedding them more deeply (primacy).

3. The **last few items** are retained in short-term memory (recency).

4. Information in the middle tends to fade or be ignored due to lack of encoding strength.

5. Judgments, choices, or recollections are disproportionately based on early and late items.

This process is largely automatic unless deliberately counteracted.

Application

- **Hiring**: Candidates interviewed first or last are more likely to be remembered and favoured.

- **Education**: Teachers can place critical content at the beginning or end of lessons to maximize retention.

- **Marketing**: First and last products in a list or shelf lineup receive more attention and higher recall.

- **Public speaking**: Speakers often craft strong openings and closings because audiences remember these most.

Key Insights

- The heuristic emphasizes **position over content** in memory and influence.

- It reveals a **predictable bias** in human recall and evaluation.

- Awareness of this effect allows better **information structuring**, such as placing important messages at the start and end.

- It can be **exploited or corrected** depending on intention— useful in persuasion, but problematic in fairness-based judgments.

- The middle is often neglected, yet may contain the most **balanced or nuanced** information.

In essence, the Serial Position Heuristic teaches us that **what comes first and last often matters more than everything in between.**

I hope you have enjoyed this book as much as I have enjoyed researching it.

On the next page you can find the other books in this series.

My best to you, Dan

OTHER BOOKS IN THIS 100 SERIES – SCAN HERE

100 COGNITIVE AND MENTAL MODELS TO HELP YOUR CAREER: Mental Shortcuts for Smarter Choices, Sharper Thinking, and Success

-

ANOTHER 100 MENTAL MODELS TO HELP YOUR CAREER - VOLUME 2: Another 100 Powerful Mental Models for Clarity, Confidence, and Climbing the Career Ladder

-

100 HEURISTICS AND HEURISTIC MODELS: The Hidden Rules of Smart Thinking Used by Experts, Entrepreneurs, and Machines

-

100 GAME THEORIES AND DECISION MODELS FOR RATIONAL DECISION MAKING IN COMPETITIVE SITUATIONS: 100 Winning Strategies for Rational Thinking in High-Stakes Scenarios

-

100 BUSINESS STRATEGIES PROVEN TACTICS FOR GROWTH, INNOVATION AND MARKET DOMINATION:

Actionable Strategies to Scale, Disrupt and Lead in Any Industry

-

<u>100 LEADERSHIP MODELS AND STRATEGIES FOR EFFECTIVE DECISION-MAKING FOR ORGANIZATIONAL SUCCESS:</u> Empowering Your Leadership, 100 Proven Strategies and Models to Enhance Decision-Making & Drive Success

-

<u>100 BUSINESS GROWTH HACKS AND STRATEGIES TO GROW PROFIT AND INCREASE YOUR COMPETITIVE ADVANTAGE:</u> Proven Techniques to Scale Faster, Boost Revenue, and Dominate Your Market with Actionable Growth

-

<u>100 ECONOMIC THEORIES DEMYSTIFIED :</u> A Guide To The World's Most Influential Economic Ideas From Keynesian Economics To Debt-deflation Theory

-

<u>100 PASSIVE INCOME STREAM SIDE HUSTLES, MASTERING SIDE HUSTLES AND SMART INVESTMENTS:</u> How to Make Money While You Sleep and Secure Your Financial Future

-

WHILST YOU ARE HERE , WHY NOT SCAN THIS TO SEE IF THERE ARE ANY MORE BOOKS PUBLISHED YET

OR FOLLOW ME AT @DANDANMUSICMAN ON X AND @DANDANMUSICMANUK ON INSTAGRAM

100 HEURISTICS + HEURISTIC MODELS

THE HIDDEN RULES OF SMART THINKING USED BY EXPERTS, ENTREPRENEURS, AND MACHINES

100 HEURISTIC MODELS

BY DAN WAITE

BRANCH AND BOUND	VORONOI	MANHATTAN DISTANCE
A* SEARCH	MINIMAX	METAHEURISTICS
SERIAL POSITION	CONTEXT-DEPENDENT	MNEMONIC
RETRIEVAL FLUENCY	SPACED REPETITION	CHUNKING
ADVERSE SELECTION	RULE CHAINING HEURISTIC	MEANS-ENDS ANALYSIS
NORM-FOLLOWING	IN-GROUP BIAS	LEFT-HAND RULE
LEFT-HAND RULE	NAVIGATION AND SPATIAL	EUCLIDEAN DISTANCE
SALIENCE	BASE RATE NEGLECT	AND MANY, MANY MORE

SIDE HUSTLES

MASTERING SIDE HUSTLES AND SMART INVESTMENTS

BY DAN WAITE

SLEEP & MEDITATION SOUNDTRACKS	RENTING OUT DRONES	LONG-TERM BONDS
SOLAR FARM INVESTMENTS	AIRBNB RENTAL ARBITRAGE	SUBSCRIPTION BASED FINANCIAL SERVICES
INVESTING IN TIMBERLAND	AUTOMATED E-COMMERCE	HEDGE FUNDS
PUBLISHING AUDIOBOOKS	AI-POWERED SEO WEBSITES	AUTOMATED PLATFORMS MONEY LENDING
AMAZON FBA BUSINESS	YOUTUBE AUTOMATION CHANNELS	FRANCHISING
TAX LIEN INVESTING	SILENT PARTNERSHIPS	CASHBACK APPS

100 PASSIVE INCOME STREAM GENERATING IDEAS

ELECTRIC BIKE RENTAL STATIONS	AIRPORT PARKING SPACE RENTAL	AUTOMATED BIKE SCOOTER RENTALS
DRONE RENTALS	SEMI-TRUCK LEASING	SOLAR PANEL LEASING
ICE VENDING MACHINES	ARCADE MACHINES	BILLBOARD SPACE
LAUNDROMATS	STORAGE FACILITY OWNERSHIP	ATM MACHINES
SAAS BUSINESS	STOCK MUSIC SALES	PRINT-ON-DEMAND
WEBSITE FLIPPING	YOUTUBE ADS	COACHING PROGRAMS
AI-GENERATED CONTENT	STOCK VIDEO FOOTAGE SALES	SELF-PUBLISHING BOOKS
VENDING MACHINES	OLD COURSE ROYALTIES	AND MANY, MANY MORE

100 BUSINESS STRATEGIES

PROVEN TACTICS FOR GROWTH, INNOVATION, AND MARKET DOMINATION

BY DAN WAITE

REFERRAL PROGRAM STRATEGY	CUSTOMER-CENTRIC STRATEGY	BOOTSTRAPPING STRATEGY
VENTURE CAPITAL STRATEGY	CROWDFUNDING STRATEGY	PRIVATE EQUITY STRATEGY
DEFENSIVE STRATEGY	HYPERLOCAL STRATEGY	DROPSHIPPING STRATEGY
AUTOMATION STRATEGY	SURPRISE & DELIGHT STRATEGY	HYPERAUTOMATION STRATEGY
REVERSE LOGISTICS STRATEGY	SIX SIGMA STRATEGY	GAMIFICATION STRATEGY
HYPER-PERSONALIZATION STRATEGY	ECOSYSTEM STRATEGY	JUST-IN-TIME (JIT) STRATEGY

100 BUSINESS STRATEGIES

BLUE OCEAN EXPANSION	BLOCKCHAIN STRATEGY	UPSELLING STRATEGY
WEB3 STRATEGY	METAVERSE STRATEGY	SEO STRATEGY
BLUE OCEAN STRATEGY	GLOBAL EXPANSION STRATEGY	CONGLOMERATE STRATEGY
HORIZONTAL INTEGRATION	VERTICAL INTEGRATION	FIRST-MOVER ADVANTAGE
FAST-FOLLOWER STRATEGY	PLATFORM STRATEGY	COST LEADERSHIP STRATEGY
DIFFERENTIATION STRATEGY	ORGANIC GROWTH STRATEGY	GROWTH HACKING STRATEGY
OMNICHANNEL STRATEGY	LOYALTY PROGRAM STRATEGY	VIRAL MARKETING STRATEGY
STORYTELLING STRATEGY	NOSTALGIA MARKETING STRATEGY	AND MANY, MANY MORE

GAME THEORY

100 GAME THEORIES AND DECISION MODELS

BY DAN WAITE

MUTUALLY ASSURED DESTRUCTION	DOLLAR AUCTION	HAWK-DOVE GAME
VOLUNTEER'S DILEMMA	SILENT DUEL	AI ALIGNMENT GAME
BAYESIAN GAME	TIPPING POINT GAME	SOCIAL INFLUENCE
TIT-FOR-TAT IN EVOLUTION	DIVIDE THE DOLLAR GAME	MONTY HALL PROBLEM
DIFFUSION OF RESPONSIBILITY	FREE RIDER PROBLEM	FLOCKING BEHAVIOUR
PARASITE-HOST GAME	CYBERSECURITY GAME	PREDATOR-PREY GAME

100 GAME THEORIES

RATIONAL DECISION-MAKING IN COMPETITIVE SITUATIONS

EVOLUTIONARILY STABLE STRATEGY	LIMITED WAR GAME	SECURITY DILEMMA
TRUST GAME	SUNK COST GAME	SHAPLEY VALUE
TERRORIST VS. GOVERNMENT	SPY VS. SPY GAME	DETERRENCE THEORY GAME
COLONEL BLOTTO GAME	WAR OF ATTRITION	MARKET FOR LEMONS
MORAL HAZARD GAME	PRINCIPAL-AGENT PROBLEM	JOB MARKET SIGNALLING
SOCIAL MEDIA VIRALITY GAME	SPAM DETECTION GAME	ADVERSE SELECTION GAME
BERTRAND COMPETITION	CASCADING FAILURE GAME	EL FAROL BAR PROBLEM
SELF-DRIVING CAR DILEMMA GAMES	MECHANISM DESIGN THEORY	AND MANY, MANY MORE